Using Literature in the Elementary Classroom

Using Literature in the Elementary Classroom

Revised and Enlarged Edition

Edited by

John Warren Stewig
University of Wisconsin–Milwaukee

Sam Leaton Sebesta
University of Washington

National Council of Teachers of English
1111 Kenyon Road, Urbana, Illinois 61801

Staff Editor: Michelle Sanden Johlas

Cover Design: Dick Maul

Interior Design: Tom Kovacs for TGK Design

NCTE Stock Number 56185-3020

Library of Congress Cataloging-in-Publication Data

Using literature in the elementary classroom / edited by John Warren Stewig, Sam Leaton Sebesta. — Rev. and enl. ed.
   p. cm.
  Includes bibliographies.
  ISBN 0-8141-5618-5
  1. Literature—Study and teaching (Elementary) I. Stewig, John Warren. II. Sebesta, Sam Leaton.
LB1575.U83 1989
372.64044—dc20

89-34680
CIP

Contents

Preface

When the first edition of *Using Literature in the Elementary Classroom* appeared in 1978, few of us knew terms such as *kid-watching, ethnography,* or *whole language*. Many of us were concerned, however, about the fragmentation of reading into several hundred skills. We wondered if reading, like Humpty Dumpty, could ever be put together again. We wondered whether reading instruction should be separated so often from the other language arts and from the rest of the curriculum, including the humanities. And we wondered why teachers' objectives had to be defined so rigorously without recourse to emergent learning and to learners' own objectives.

A decade later each of these concerns has been addressed by Julie M. Jensen, incoming president of the National Council of Teachers of English. She cites "heartening evidence" of change. She finds "strengthened links" among the language arts, a broader and more humanizing view of assessment, and greater faith in "local control" that empowers teachers. And in the February 1989 issue of *Language Arts,* she points to "a growing role of children's literature in elementary school classrooms." It's an optimistic view, and one hopes that it will be further justified and sustained in the 1990s.

Opinion has changed and with it, some school practices, as evidenced by theoretical and anecdotal articles in *Language Arts* and other periodicals. The movement is toward child-centered, problem-oriented instruction (John Dewey called it "experimentalism"). It is toward holistic or integrated skills and subject areas. In some aspects at least, it is a movement toward a literature-based curriculum. If the movement is to survive, it must grow and change. It must, above all, find expertise—not just from a handful of enthusiastic specialists but from the army of educators on the front lines, daily in the schools.

Hence, we offer this new edition—not so much to describe the change as to help implement it. Application is the keynote. Here you'll find a collection of books almost guaranteed to start a fascination with vocabulary. You'll find explication of the tie between words and the rich visual imagery of picture books. The holistic connection of visual and oral literacy to critical examination of pictures is explored by an expert. We learn the distinctive features of genres, including those of nonfiction as well as fiction, with explicit ideas for developing self-questioning and metacognition using these naturally occurring texts.

The response-to-literature studies of the past two decades have made us aware that a kaleidoscope of response modes applies to the literature program. From discussion comes creative dramatics, visual arts, and writing. (You'll find here tantalizing lists of writing activities to enhance literary experience.) There is an effort to illustrate ways that children's literature can supplement or become the center of content-area teaching.

No one attempts to lay all this on a procrustean taxonomy of objectives or learning compartments, for it is recognized that books, activities, and outcomes merge. But you will find repeated mention of two aspects of education that have been neglected. One is that of feeding the *imagination*: the wellspring of creativity, the active mind, and self-motivation. The other is that of *valuing*: learning to make wise choices, whether in deciding what to read or what to *do*.

In one of the chapters, Mary Jett-Simpson weighs the evidence on whether drama activities effectively promote comprehension of literature. This question has been further explored in *Language Arts* by Betty Jane Wagner. The question and present evidence are of wide interest, for the answer seems to be yes, no, and maybe. *Some* drama applications yield good results, *some* do not. Why the difference? If we were to explore the outcomes of all applications of activities to literature described in this book, what would the results be? The next decade will likely provide better answers, but for the time being, two observations regarding the broadened, holistic approach to using literature in the classroom seem warranted. The first is that technique must be fostered. Drama isn't likely to work if it is left to happen without skill and guidance. "Draw a picture of the story" is less likely to prove the value of visual imagery activity than imaginative presentation of visual arts options. Hence the need for training, planning, and guidance from specialists such as the authors cited as references in these chapters.

The second observation is made by Jett-Simpson: that present assessment may ignore most important outcomes. A "facts" test may stop short of assessing understanding. A test of reading comprehension alone will not tell us whether the readers *want* to comprehend, will go on to seek to comprehend, and are on their way to becoming mature, voluntary readers. Veridical ongoing assessment becomes a partner of innovative use of literature described in these pages.

Those who would use literature in the elementary classroom must know children's books. Knowing this and feeling their own enthusiasm, chapter authors in this volume have been generous with titles. You'll find books suggested for classroom use, related or additional readings, and references listed at the end of each chapter. You'll note that some titles have gone out of print. That's not our fault! Remember, out-of-print titles may still be found in libraries and personal collections. Remember, too, that no book in this growing, changing field can ever be quite up-to-date. This moment, as you read this page, a new children's book may have appeared, perfect for using with the ideas on page XX. Don't miss it, and don't forget to share your find!

Sam Leaton Sebesta
University of Washington

Introduction

In the decade since the first edition of this book was published, there has been a revolution in literacy instruction in the schools. Changes began to occur slowly in isolated locations, then became more widespread as teachers embraced a new way of thinking about literacy and the means to encourage it. In recent years the changes have finally resulted in an enthusiastic movement.

Those of us interested in using books to enhance literacy are encouraged that many voices are reinforcing the point of view expressed in this volume's first edition, a view that places literature, real books by real authors, at the center of instruction. Moving beyond narrow definitions of skill development in rigid sequences, teachers—with the help of sympathetic local administrators and strong voices in state departments of education—are establishing literacy environments. A central part of these settings, in addition to the children's own language, is the uncut and unchanged language of authors in books. And so this book, updated and expanded, becomes even more critical.

The book originated at the 1976 Anaheim convention of the International Reading Association, where all the contributors were program participants. The authors are a diverse group: they come from different backgrounds and work in different sorts of literacy-related jobs, yet share a common belief that literature should be used to help children develop the skills so necessary to survival in today's complex world.

Each of the writers has been an elementary classroom teacher, and in the time since leaving that as a full-time job, each has spent many hours in schools working with teachers and children. A common concern is finding ways to build on the language ability children bring with them to school, so that they will read with sureness and strength—taking in the author's written words, understanding and interpreting them effectively. One of the key ways to do this is to make sure that a significant part of the school reading program is a planned, sequential literature strand which involves all children.

There are those who question using literature for anything. Some experts assert that literature should just "be," should be shared with children incidentally for whatever they choose to take from it, and should not be organized into instructional sequences. Indeed literature can be abused, when it is not carefully studied and then thoughtfully incorporated into a sensitively developed sequence of experiences which respects the integrity of each book. Each author of this volume shares a deep concern for literature, and each chapter conveys that feeling. Sharing our appreciation of literature with children is the context from which we propose specific books and the techniques for using them.

A danger in books featuring writing by various authors is that in the end, the efforts remain separate: disparate ideas by different people. That problem is mitigated here by the fact that these seven authors share a common philosophy about the use of books with children. In addition to this intrinsic link between chapters, the editors have provided an extrinsic link: headnotes relate each chapter to those that precede it.

The book opens with A. Barbara Pilon's chapter on the study of language, for what is more fundamental to a broad-based literacy than understanding the scope of the language we speak? Simple decoding skills are not enough if children remain unaware of and unresponsive to the range and diversity of the language they are decoding.

Alden J. Moe's chapter focuses on very young children learning to read. On the basis of his research into vocabulary loads in picture books, the author makes a practical appeal for initial reading instruction based on these books. Teachers will find that the vocabulary load of each book is indicated, an invaluable tool in picking fine literature that is also within the language ability of the child reader.

Helen Felsenthal devotes her attention to older children who have already mastered basic decoding skills. These children are ready for wider-ranging examination of literature, including the use of non-fiction as a way of expanding literacy skills.

In the following chapter, John Warren Stewig suggests venturing away from print, to develop visual and verbal literacy skills—two stepchildren in the language/reading curriculum. Children come to school with eyes open at the wonder of the world around them; they talk copiously about what they have perceived visually. Unfortunately, concern with helping children in receptive literacy—learning to read—too frequently inhibits the development of these visual/oral literacy skills.

Two other authors recommend branching out from the center of basic programs, to involve children in related experiences that enhance a wider definition of literacy. Richard G. Kolczynski examines the nature of the composition process, particularly as it relates to literature as motivational input. By helping children develop their expressive literacy skills, we also improve the reading instruction we offer them. In addition, Mary Jett-Simpson shows us ways teachers can use informal classroom drama to enhance and assess children's comprehension abilities. These techniques are equally effective as more traditional paper-and-pencil ways to understanding.

To conclude the book, Sam Leaton Sebesta looks at literature across the curriculum, pointing out ways teachers can use books in a variety of content areas. The approach to literature which these authors share is not limited to the literacy development part of the curriculum, but also can be used to enrich the study of such areas as science, social studies, and art, among others.

Many people have commented that it is not enough to teach children how to read; we must, in addition, teach children to *want* to read. With the feeling that traditional reading programs often teach children how to read, but do not instill the *desire* to read, we have prepared this enlarged edition. It is our belief that the techniques described here do go beyond basic reading instruction to the wider definitions of literacy that produce greater interest in reading.

John Warren Stewig
University of Wisconsin–
Milwaukee

1 Reading to Learn about the Nature of Language

A. Barbara Pilon
Worcester State College

"Contagious" often has a pejorative meaning, but it can also describe a kind of enthusiasm. In this chapter, A. Barbara Pilon reveals a contagious enthusiasm for words and their unique qualities.

The author is a word-o-phile, delighting in the history, derivations, unusual meanings, peculiarities, and possibilities of words. She sees each one as individual and believes that knowing words intimately helps children expand their reading-language power.

Pilon shares her fascination with words through the books she recommends and the activities she suggests. She hopes that teachers, too, will be motivated to help children develop this delight in words.

Some time ago, Walter Petty called for increased development of teaching techniques beyond the isolated study of word lists (*The State of Knowledge about the Teaching of Vocabulary*, 1968; Urbana, Ill.: National Council of Teachers of English). This important summary of research about vocabulary and how it is taught remains important today, when word-list teaching is still unfortunately commonplace. Pilon responds by suggesting practical ideas for children's word study as they work toward increased proficiency in language and reading.

Our language is calorie-rich. We are a nation unafraid of borrowing. We have never penalized our citizens in any way (as have the French, for example), for using words from another nation. In our adoption of foreign terms, as was said of Shakespeare, we invade like conquerors. There is much that children can learn about the nature of language through reading.

Importance of imagination. Since language itself is fluid, chameleon-like, and has an unlimited potential for change and growth, children can be helped to see that imagination (what Jan Carew [1974] has called "the third gift") is the most important element in talking about our language.

1

Delight and magic of words. Helping children realize the delight and the magic of words should be one of our foremost goals as language arts and reading teachers. If we can accomplish this, then many children will become "word gatherers," as was the title character in Leo Lionni's charming book *Frederick* (1973).

Influence of words on all of us. Children also should become aware of the influence that words have upon all of us. We want our youngsters to be like Patricia Hubbell's Word Woman, who carries words with her in a jar, threading them to stars when she wants to travel (1958). We want them to be able to create, to soar and fly with language.

Teachers can explore with children, using books suggested at the end of this chapter, to discover new vistas of the wonders and joys of language. Supplemental activities are described for teachers to use in conjunction with the books. Characteristics about language that are discussed include:

1. Linguists all: the great potential for growth in language
2. Changes, changes: the Protean nature of words
3. The arbitrariness of language
4. The role of intonation in language
5. Punctuation makes a difference: the role of juncture in language

Linguists All: The Great Potential for Growth in Language

To show children how new words have come into our language, make up worksheets containing lists of words that have come to us from other languages. This helps children see the eclectic nature of our language. The papers can be divided into columns to show Spanish, French, Italian, German, Native American, African, and other words that we have assimilated into English. Children can be encouraged to add to the lists, including the origins of their own names. Such an exercise is bound to enhance children's self-concepts, since they will realize how many "foreign" words they know.

If we are to excite children about the "languages" they already know, then teachers must set the spark. Take familiar words—words dear to children's hearts and stomachs. Ask students if these are American words, then tell them where the words came from. Some to begin with might be:

1. *dungaree*—a Hindi word for cotton cloth called *dungri* (Epstein 1964, 35).

2. *denim*—comes from France, specifically from the name of a city, Nîmes. The word is short for *serge de Nîmes.*

3. *jeans*—comes to us from Genoa and is short for the Italian term *jean fustian.* The sailors in Genoa wore clothes made from this kind of material. Incidentally, jeans are also called *Levi's,* a word derived from the name of the man responsible for making Levi's so popular in this country. Words are often derived from people's names and this method of originating new terms should be made known to children. A fine resource to help children become acquainted with eponyms is Bill Severn's *People Words* (1966).

4. *hamburger*—from Hamburg, Germany.

5. *frankfurter*—from Frankfurt, Germany.

6. *chocolate*—from the Mexican Aztec word *chocolatl* (Epstein 1964, 35).

7. *candy*—comes from the ancient language Sanskrit, once spoken in India. The Sanskrit word is *khanda,* which simply meant "piece," but was frequently employed to refer to a piece of sugar (Epstein 1964, 33–34).

8. *cafeteria*—coffee shop, from Spanish *café* (coffee).

After students have explored different books about word origins, give them lists including such words as *disaster, television,* and *astronaut,* and ask them to attempt a logical explanation of the words' meanings. Afterward they can consult the etymologies in dictionaries. This kind of exercise shows children one way in which language grows. In addition, it may stir a curiosity for studying the etymologies of words. This is just what we are hoping for!

Other ways to show children the great elastic potential of language are the use of:

1. *Coined words.* Gelett Burgess made up his own dictionary called *Burgess Unabridged.* It contained 600 words he thought were needed in the English language. One word found in current dictionaries is one Burgess created: *blurb* (Ferguson 1964, 31). Children will enjoy making up some needed words of their own if they are given encouragement to do so. At this point, for instance, no one has offered a satisfactory nonsexist word that can be used in such sentences as "Each of the children went to HIS seat."

2. *Portmanteau words,* or blends. Lewis Carroll is famous for his use of portmanteau words in *Alice in Wonderland.* A portmanteau

word (*portmanteau* itself is a French term and literally means to carry a mantle) consists of putting two words together to make a new word, while leaving out some of the original letters. Some blends we use today, probably without thinking of the two words from which they came, are *bash* (bat and mash), *clash* (clap and crash), *flare* (flame and glare), and *glimmer* (gleam and shimmer) (Farb 1973, 351–52). Other portmanteau words include *motel, brunch,* and *smog.* Let students collect old dictionaries to find out if these words appear in them. Children enjoy making up their own portmanteau words. Provide some examples to get them started. Some I tried were: "submersed" in work, "innumbdated" with things to do, and a "clousy" day. One good book for children to look at which includes some patchwords is *Dandelions Don't Bite* by Leone Adelson (1972).

3. *"Slide" words.* Slide words, as I term them, have come into existence either by putting two letters or a letter and a word together to make one new word. Examples of slide words are *jeep* and *blimp. Jeep* originally was used by G.I.s during World War II to describe a "general purpose" vehicle. Later the initials "G.P." were painted on the vehicles, and soldiers "slid" the letters together to get the word *jeep. Blimp* came to us from the English, who were attempting to create "limp" airships during World War I. Their "A-limp" model didn't work out, but their "B-limp" did. Eureka, *blimp* became part of our vocabulary (Miller 1974, 8 and 24).

4. *Slanguage.* This is a portmanteau word, used to describe the way words take on new meaning in our vocabularies, extending and enriching language. In talking with children about our language, give them examples of such words as *cool, bad, mean, tough, dough,* and *hot.* Ask the class what the standard meanings of those words are, and how they think these words took on their present, colloquial meanings. Let them add to the list of slanguage words. When children consult various modern dictionaries to see whether the slang meanings are included, they realize that one aspect of language is its changeability.

5. *Brand words* derived from trademarks, such as *zipper, nylon, Ping-Pong, Band-Aid, Xerox,* and *Formica.* Have children note that the more deeply embedded a word becomes in our language, the more casually we treat it. We can expect, thus, that one day soon all of these words will have lost their capital letters. Suggest to children that they look in different dictionaries to see whether

certain words appear in them. The words *Xerox* and *Formica*, for example, did not appear at all in the 1950 edition of *Webster's New Collegiate Dictionary*. Children may be amazed to find out that within a short time, new words evolve and become important parts of our vocabulary. In addition to brand names, new medical discoveries, unusual events, inventions, and social changes necessitate creation of new words. If the children are old enough, discuss terms they know that have either come into usage recently or have new meanings attached to them. They can discuss how and why these new words were created. Have them look at old dictionaries to see whether the words *transplant* and *pacemaker* (with their medical meanings), *splashdown, skyjack,* and *snowmobile* appear. Through such an activity, children come to realize that some dictionaries in today's classrooms most certainly do not contain words that many people will be acquainted with in the year 2001!

6. *Acronyms.* These are words formed from the first letters of the words in a compound term. For example, our word *radar* comes from the phrase "*ra*dio *de*tecting *a*nd *r*anging." Other examples include *snafu, posh, scuba,* and *laser.*

7. *People words.* Initiate curiosity about words that have come to us from people, real or imaginary. Tell students the origins of the words *tantalize, Pluto* (ask children why they think Walt Disney named his famous dog Pluto), and *Europe* (reading Greek legends such as Nathaniel Hawthorne's classic *Tanglewood Tales* will help give children an appreciation of the words mentioned). Other words with fascinating "people" histories, which may serve as a starter list for pupils, include *cereal, chauvinism, mercury, volcano, January, Mars, bloomer, sandwich, pasteurize, gerrymander, guillotine, cardigan, raglan, spoonerism,* and *boycott.* Nancy Sorel's *Word People* (1970) and Bill Severn's *People Words* (1966) help children with some of these words.

8. *Prefixes, suffixes,* and *compound words.* Many new words are incorporated into our language by the technique of adding prefixes or suffixes to root words and by putting two root words together to form new words.

The point of the foregoing suggestions is to demonstrate the many strategies we employ to increase our language. Children should understand that *people* create language and therefore, *they* are capable of adding words to our English language. They can be the creators; they can be the makers of our music, not just the recipients. By working with some of these same techniques, children come to understand that one aspect of language is its ability to expand infinitely.

Changes, Changes: The Protean Nature of Words

An important facet of language is that it constantly changes sounds and meanings.

Euphemisms

Words and phrases change because people feel it is necessary to "pretty up" language. A garbage collector now is called a sanitary engineer, an undertaker is a mortician, a hairdresser is a beautician (Tiedt and Tiedt 1975, 134), and the Vietnam War has been referred to as an international armed conflict (Farb 1973, 155). For further interesting reading about euphemisms, you may wish to look at Edwin Newman's *Strictly Speaking* (1974). Newman argues that the purpose of tampering with a word or phrase is often to obfuscate and conceal its true meaning.

Etymologies

By studying the etymologies of words, children learn that location, time, and people affect the meanings and pronunciations of words. Lively discussions occur as children are told, for example, that *queen* once meant simply "woman" (Miller 1974, 39). *Girl* meant a "young person" (McCormack 1967, 29); it did not make any difference whether the person was male or female. (Since *girl* was once a nonsexist word, perhaps its original meaning should be adopted again.) *Female*, too, was originally *femelle*, a nonsexist word which meant "small woman," but because of its obvious resemblance to the word *male*, it was changed to what it is today (Farb 1973, 161).

Sometimes words start out with rather inoffensive meanings and change to offensive ones, or vice versa. For instance, *idiot* once meant "an ignorant person," while *nice* meant "ignorant or foolish." As mentioned previously, changes in meaning are occurring continually in slang. A word such as *heavy*, which could carry a negative meaning in our slanguage, now can have a positive tone.

Sometimes we hear a word, think that a mistake has been made by the person pronouncing it, and undertake to change the word to make it "right." This is what has happened to *chaise lounge*, a French term that is actually spelled *chaise longue*—a long chair. Most people,

Imagine the CAT in CATerpillar.
An insect that purrs? Think about it.

Marms in the Marmalade by Diana Morley, illustrated by Kathy Rogers, copyright 1984. Reproduced by permission of the publisher, Carolrhoda Books, 241 First Avenue North, Minneapolis, MN 55401.

however, refer to it as a *chaise lounge,* a logical change in pronunciation and spelling since it does reflect the function of the chair (Farb 1973, 352–53). Examples of foreign words that we anglicize in pronunciation and spelling are *dandelion*—French *dent de lion* (teeth of the lion), and *royal*—Spanish *real.*

Unusual Processes in English

In English there is a process by which a noun drops the letter *n* it originally had and adds it to the article preceding it. Examples of such words are *an orange* (originally Arabic *naranj*), *an adder* (*a nadder*), and *an apron* (*a napron*) (Farb 1973, 339–40). In *Dandelions Don't Bite,* Leone Adelson gives the background of the word *nickname*

(1972, 27). Originally, it was *an eke name* but then, in a reverse process, it became *nekename* and finally *nickname.*

Losses

People tend either to drop unstressed parts of a word or phrase or to telescope them. This process of loss is evident if one is aware that originally the words *pants, cab, piano,* and *nob,* for example, were *pantalone* (after a fifteenth-century comedian), *cabriolet, pianoforte,* and *nabob.* As individuals become familiar with terms, too, there is a tendency to shorten them. Thus, *television* becomes *TV, David* becomes *Dave, day's eye* becomes *daisy, all one* becomes *alone,* and *by cause of* becomes *because* (Adelson 1972, 27).

Flexibility

After reading books such as the delightful *Amelia Bedelia* series by Peggy Parish, children will be conscious that many words in English are multinyms or homophones—words that are spelled alike and sound alike but have different meanings. Words such as *box, shower, bark, trunk,* and *run* all have multiple definitions and do change their meanings depending on the context. Children enjoy extending the stories about Amelia, a silly maid but wonderful cook who, because of her emaciated vocabulary, is always getting into trouble. Amelia invariably has a meaning for a word, but unfortunately, it is always the inappropriate one. Children find her misinterpretations hilarious.

Two books that can exercise children's logic as well as their vocabulary powers are *A Gaggle of Geese* (1960) and *Small Fry* (1965), both by Eve Merriam. These books explain what units of animals are called. Children can be asked why they think a group of lions is called a pride, or why a group of bears is called a sloth. Have children define different assemblages of people and see if they can give logical attributes to the groups they are describing. Some students, when given this exercise, responded by creating the following collective words:

> an ooze of bricklayers
> a school of teachers
> a muttering of mothers
> a seat of secretaries
> a gam of girls

Teachers of older children will find useful *An Exaltation of Larks,* by James Lipton (1968).

The Arbitrariness of Language

Another aspect of language is its arbitrariness, not only when we refer to the words or lexicon of a language, but also when we refer to its syntax or structure. An easy way to demonstrate this is to tell children that although we call a dog a *dog*, in German the same animal is labeled *hund*, in Spanish it is *perro*, and in Italian it is *cane*. Any good dictionary can supply other examples.

In introducing children to books that demonstrate the arbitrariness of language, teachers should select materials that show a story or poem in English and other languages. One fine resource that discusses four Spanish-English books, all published by Children's Book Press in 1986 and 1987, is included on pages 89–91 in the January/February 1988 issue of *The Horn Book*.

By working with materials such as these and the dual language books recommended at the end of this chapter, children can be led to see not only the arbitrariness of language, but the fluency, inventiveness, and creativity of its makers.

The Role of Intonation in Language

Almost everyone is capable of understanding early in life that how you say something is as important as what you say. Hearing someone say, "That's lovely, isn't it?" is very different from reading the same words. By listening, we know whether the person speaking is being sincere or sarcastic. Reading does not provide as many clues to its receivers as oral language does. Thus, intonation clues are a great boon to comprehending what is meant. Certain books are especially valuable because they allow pupils an opportunity to have fun with language while gaining insight into the purpose of intonation.

Another idea in working with intonation is to introduce children to wordless picture books. A complete consideration of such books is presented by Zena Sutherland and May Hill Arbuthnot in *Children and Books* (1986, 101–103 and 121). Let the children, either alone or in small groups, decide upon captions for the pictures. Then they can present their versions of the book, utilizing their intonation skills as well as all their other language skills.

One book children enjoy working with is *The Elephant's Visit* (Warner 1975). Another suggestion is *The Joneses* (Ramage 1975). Although it does have six words on the first page—"Have a good day, dear husband!"—the rest of the book is wordless. The story tells of a family consisting of thirty-one children (one a dragon child), a mother who drives a submarine, and a father who stays home and takes care of the family. It would be good for two children to tell this story, since for most of the book the left-hand side shows what is going on at home while the right side depicts what is happening to the mother.

Other excellent wordless picture books have been created by Martha Alexander, Ruth Carroll, John Goodall, Mercer Mayer, Emily Arnold McCully, and Fernando Krahn.

Punctuation Makes a Difference: The Role of Juncture in Language

Where we pause when we speak and how long we pause can make all the difference in the messages we are trying to convey. Howie Schneider, in a cartoon "The Circus of P. T. Bimbo" (NEA 1975), makes it clear that it is important, when advertising for an employee, to distinguish between a TIGHT rope walker and a TIGHTROPE walker. There is a difference, too, in the following two statements:

> You should sit down before you eat Mother.

> You should sit down before you eat, Mother.

Students enjoy making up and sharing their own sentences which prove that juncture markers are critical. Before asking them to do this, however, work with them on some juncture exercises.

In these and other ways, as children read they learn about the nature of language. As we share the books recommended here and plan the suggested activities, children learn the delight of words. They come to understand the words of Emily Dickinson, who wrote:

> A word is dead
> When it is said,
> Some say.

> I say it just
> Begins to live
> That day.

Recommended Books for Classroom Use

These annotated booklists, organized by topic, provide background on and suggestions for using the recommended books in the classroom.

An asterisk (*) before an entry indicates that at the time the revised edition of *Using Literature in the Elementary Classroom* went to press, that particular book was out of print, according to *Books in Print*. Those books likely are still available from your local public or school library.

Word Origins

*Adelson, Leone. 1972. *Dandelions Don't Bite: The Story of Words.* New York: Pantheon.

This book helps children become interested in the origins of words. One chapter is entitled "Cousins by the Dozens." The author shows how words such as *octopus, pedal,* and *pedestrian* are related, as are *pupil, puppy, puppet; clock* and *cloak; rival* and *river; poodle* and *puddle; onion* and *union; pansy* and *pensive;* and *paper* and *papyrus.* Adelson tells her readers of many words we have received from the Greeks, including *school* (*scholé*), which meant free time! Derivations of our words *hello* ("Hale be thou," "Whole be thou") and *good-bye* ("God be with ye!") are two of the many words explained.

Adelson introduces portmanteau words such as *brunch, smog,* and *motel,* although she calls them "patchwords." She includes her own original portmanteau word, *smeeze,* which is a sneeze caused by smog and smaze (39). Teachers should encourage youngsters to create their own needed new words which could be portmanteau words.

Ames, Winthrop, editor. 1974. *What Shall We Name the Baby?* New York: Pocket Books.

Children will enjoy exploring this paperback to find out what their names and their friends' names mean. If children don't like their names, let them make up new names for themselves and share with classmates what their new names mean.

*Boyer, Sophia A., and Winifred Lubell. 1970. *Gifts from the Greeks: Alpha to Omega.* Chicago: Rand McNally.

Interesting word etymologies are given, including those for *hypocrite,* which originally meant "actor"; *gymnastics* and *gymnasium,* derived from the Greek word *gymnos,* which meant "naked"; and *idiot* from *idiotes,* which meant a citizen who did not participate in politics.

*Epstein, Beryl, and Sam Epstein. 1964. *What's Behind the Word?* New York: Scholastic.

This paperback includes information on how writing began, how modern English (1500 to today) has borrowed words from all over the world, how new words are made from old, what spoonerisms are, and how we get words that are derived from people's names (eponyms), though the Epsteins do not use this term.

Hall, Rich, and Friends. 1984. *Sniglets—Any Word that Doesn't Appear in the Dictionary, But Should.* New York: Macmillan.

In this series of paperbacks—*More Sniglets* (1985), *Angry Young Sniglets* (1987), *Sniglets for Kids: Sniglets Collector Sticker Books* (1985), and *More Sniglets for Kids* (1986)—the authors give us new words such as *nurge,* "to inch closer to a stoplight thinking that will cause it to change quicker" (1984, 58), and *telletiquette,* "the polite distance kept by one person behind another at an automatic teller machine" (1984, 81). The books aimed at children are targeted for grades three through seven.

Hazen, Barbara Shook. 1979. *Last, First, Middle and Nick: All About Names.* Englewood Cliffs, N.J.: Prentice-Hall.

Children enjoy browsing in this selection. One section asks them to match last names with what the names say about the persons; e.g., Kennedy is bigheaded, Doolittle is lazy, and Truman is a trusted hardworker. Hazen lists the fifty most common surnames (Smith, followed by Johnson, tops the list) and recounts intriguing facts such as, "In Iceland, people are listed by their first names in the phone book."

*Kohn, Bernice. 1974. *What a Funny Thing to Say!* New York: Dial.

The introductory chapter lists collective nouns for animals, such as "a skulk of foxes" and "a gang of buffalo." For other sources that deal with collective nouns, consult Brian Wildsmith's beautifully illustrated *Birds* (1967), *Fishes* (1968), and *Wild Animals* (1986).

Be sure to show students how authors make their own collective words for things and let children try to do the same thing. For this purpose, note Adrienne Adams's title for *A Woggle of Witches* (Aladdin, 1985) and L. M. Boston's references to "a parliament of badgers" and "a litany of worms" in *The River at Green Knowe* (Peter Smith, 1984). In her third chapter, Kohn also shows her readers "How to Make a Word."

Meltzer, Milton. 1984. *A Book about Names.* New York: Crowell.

Meltzer tells readers the meanings of many last names. For instance, Kelly means "contentious," Riley means "playful," Burke means "dweller at the fort," and Murphy means "the sea-fighter." Many German surnames are presented and translated, e.g., Weintraub, "grape"; Strauss, "ostrich"; Schultz, "carter"; Adler, "eagle"; and Weber, "weaver." Meltzer tells us that Plato, meaning "broad," received that nickname from a gymnastics teacher. His real name was Aristocles, his grandfather's name.

*Pizer, Vernon. 1976. *Ink, Ark., and All That: How American Places Got Their Names.* New York: Putnam.

Fascinating and often humorous facts about how places got their names. For instance, Ink, Arkansas, got its name when the government sent a questionnaire to each family in the-then-nameless town and on the form requested that each family "PLEASE WRITE IN INK." Most citizens complied and wrote down the word *Ink.*

Massachusetts derived its name from an Indian tribe that lived in the area around Boston. Rhode Island is generally believed to have received its name because a Dutch navigator saw the red clay on the shore and thought of the words *Roodt Eylandt,* Dutch for "a red island." Officially, though, the legal name for Rhode Island is Rhode Island and Providence Plantations. Thus, the longest name is given to the smallest state! Encourage children to investigate the names of places close to them to see if they can uncover how the names originated.

*————. 1981. *Take My Word for It.* New York: Dodd, Mead.

This book by Pizer is concerned with eponyms, a term coined from the Greek words *epi* and *onyma,* meaning "upon a name." But the word was formed "for the broader purpose of meaning the person for whom something is named!" (13). Some of the people, real and imaginary, for whom things were named are Jean Nicot (nicotine), Morpheus (morphine), Joel Robert Poinsett (poinsettia), Jules Léotard (leotards), Kid McCoy (the real McCoy), Elihu Frisbee (Frisbees), and César Ritz (ritzy).

Sarnoff, Jane, and Reynold Ruffins. 1981. *Words.* New York: Scribner's.

This is for budding word addicts. Some interesting etymologies (*etumon,* "true word," and *logio,* "study of") are:

> *boy*—male servant, or a youth or man of low birth (12)
>
> *girl*—a child of either sex (12)

Husband

Husband is a combination of an Old English word, *hus,*
from which we get the word *house,* and an Old Norse word,
bondi, 'owner'. So a husband was a houseowner. The word
was first used for all men who owned houses or were head
of the household and later for all married men.

> *man*—a human being (13)
>
> *bride*—to cook or to make broth (14)
>
> *husband*—*hus* (house) plus *bondi* (owner) (12)
>
> *woman*—prefix *wif* before *mann,* denoting gender of human
> being (13)

Steckler, Arthur. 1979. *101 Words And How They Began.* New York:
   Doubleday.

   This book for young etymologists includes many fascinating stories
about words in our language. Steckler recounts that our word *ballot*
comes from the Italian words *balla,* meaning "ball," and *ballotta,*
meaning "little ball," and that in ancient Greece, white balls were
dropped into a box if you wanted to elect a candidate, whereas a
black ball was dropped to defeat someone. In French, *boulette* means

"little hole" and from that we get *bullet*. *Magazine* comes from the Arabic word *makhazin*, which means "a storehouse."

Stewart, George R. 1979. *American Given Names*. New York: Oxford.

Here is another useful source to investigate the meanings of boys' and girls' first names.

Dual Language Books

*DuBois, William Pène. 1972. *The Hare and the Tortoise and the Tortoise and the Hare: La Liebre y la Tortuga y la Tortuga y la Liebre.* New York: Doubleday.

Two stories are presented in this book. On each page the rhyme in English has a blue background and the Spanish version has a pink background. It would help children if teachers who plan to present this book could read Spanish so that they could give a literal translation of the Spanish version of the story, which appears opposite the English version.

Feelings, Muriel. 1974. *Jambo Means Hello: Swahili Alphabet Book.* New York: Dial.

Words from *A* to *Z* are celebrated in this tradebook. There are only twenty-four letters in Swahili, as there are no *Q* or *X* sounds. As in *Moja Means One!*, the author gives each word's phonetic pronunciation in parentheses. The pictures in both books are handsome.

————. 1976. *Moja Means One! A Swahili Counting Book.* New York: Dial.

Swahili words are given in red with the phonetic pronunciation included below in parentheses. There is an introduction to this book, as well as an author's note at the end.

Griego, Margot, et al., editors and translators. 1981. *Tortillitas Para Mama: And Other Nursery Rhymes.* New York: Holt, Rinehart and Winston.

This is a collection of Latin-American nursery rhymes illustrated by Barbara Cooney. The Spanish verse is followed by the English rendition.

*Joslin, Sesyle. 1961. *There Is a Dragon in My Bed (Il y a un Dragon dans Mon Lit)*. New York: Harcourt.

A delightful book that very considerately lets its readers know phrases that are imperative to have at one's fingertips if one is traveling in France. Not only are the phrases translated and listed with the phonetic pronunciations below them, but the reader is told when the phrases should be used by means of charming illustrations.

*————. 1966. *There Is a Bull on My Balcony (Hay un Toro en Mi Balcón)*. New York: Harcourt, Brace.

Joslin playfully provides phrases in Spanish and English that are essential to know if you are planning to go to Mexico. In the previous book as well as in this one, children can supply their own phrases they feel would be needed, not only in French and Spanish but in any other languages they know.

Rosario, Idalia. 1981. *Idalia's Project ABC–Proyecto ABC: An Urban Alphabet Book in English and Spanish*. New York: Holt, Rinehart and Winston.

Includes *ch* and *li* in the alphabet and contains sentences such as, "*R* is for rats. Rats are a health hazard for all cities."

Intonation

*Brown, Marcia. 1969. *How, Hippo!* New York: Scribner's.

Little Hippo is taught by his mother the heteronym *how* in this story. *How* can mean "hello," "watch out," and "help," and Little Hippo is warned that he better learn how to roar the appropriate one. Pupils would enjoy chiming in when this is read, "roaring" their own appropriate intonations.

*McPhail, David. 1973. *Oh, No, Go*. Boston: Little, Brown.

This is a play that has only three words in it—the words in the title. Children could be encouraged to study the pictures in the book and then determine how they would say each of the words on the different pages. Some students could be stimulated to create their own books or plays using a minimum number of words.

*Mayer, Marianna, and Mercer Mayer. 1973. *Mine!* New York: Scholastic.

Mine consists of only two words—*mine* and *yours*. It should be fun for students to act out this story using the correct intonation for each word.

Punctuation

Brewton, Sara, John E. Brewton, and G. Meredith Blackburn III. 1973. *My Tang's Tungled and Other Ridiculous Situations.* New York: Crowell.

Try having children punctuate, after having deleted the author's punctuation, the poem by Morris Bishop, "Song of the Pop Bottlers." Try also the following poems, all written by unknown authors: "If a Doctor Is Doctoring a Doctor," "I Saw Esau," "Say, Did You Say?" and "The Old School Scold."

Gardner, Martin. 1988. *Perplexing Puzzles and Tantalizing Teasers.* New York: Dover.

Have students decipher the paragraph "Sally's Silly Walk" by punctuating it differently.

*Nurnberg, Maxwell. 1968. *Punctuation Pointers.* New York: Scholastic.

This little paperback is invaluable for providing boys and girls with innumerable provocative punctuation exercises. For instance, two questions dealing with commas can be found on page 56:

> In which has the speaker pried into the private lives of his friends?
> a. Everyone I know has a secret ambition.
> b. Everyone, I know, has a secret ambition.
> Which is a matter of identification?
> a. He is the one, I believe.
> b. He is the one I believe.

For creative poems concerned with punctuation marks that students will take pleasure in, be sure to look at Richard Armour's *On Your Marks: A Package of Punctuation* (1969, New York: McGraw-Hill); *Words Words Words* by Mary O'Neill (1966, New York: Doubleday; 28–31); and Eve Merriam's *Finding a Poem* (1970, New York: Atheneum; 24–28).

*———. 1970. *Fun With Words.* Englewood Cliffs, N.J.: Prentice-Hall.

Chapter Seven, "A Comedy of Commas," includes some more typical Nurnberg exercises plus some brainteasers, such as this sentence that needs a little punctuation assistance: "That that is is that that is not is not that that is not is not that that is is is that it it is." Another delightful source for working with punctuation creatively is Nora Gallagher's *How to Stop a Sentence* (1984, New York: Lippincott Junior Books).

*Withers, Carl. 1964. *A Treasury of Games.* New York: Grosset and Dunlap.

On page 125, Withers tantalizes his readers to make sense out of five different passages, e.g., "In writing paper and pencil leave space between paper and and and and and pencil." (In writing "paper and pencil," leave space between "paper" and "and" and "and" and "pencil.") Also use the poem "There were two skunks," eliminating all punctuation. It can also be found in Alvin Schwartz's *Tomfoolery* (1976, New York: Bantam).

Children's Books for Language Development

Funk, Charles Earle. 1985. *Hog on Ice and Other Curious Expressions.* New York: Harper and Row.

Expressions we use, although we may not know why, are explained in this paperback. Some sayings that are explained are: "not dry behind the ears," "worth one's salt" (the word *salary* comes from *salt*), and "a feather in his cap." This is a wonderful book to wander through. It should stimulate children's curiosity to explore other expressions they use. Also see two more books by Funk: *Heavens to Betsy!* (1986) and *Thereby Hangs a Tale* (1985).

Goffstein, M. B. 1986. *The School of Names.* New York: Harper.

This is a beautiful book which very simply states that the author wants to know every fish, every star, every rock, continent, sea, lake, desert, river, mountain, cloud, flower, etc., by name. She wishes to attend the School of Names. Children should be enticed to explore their vocabularies after being exposed to this book.

Hoberman, Mary Ann. 1978. *A House Is a House for Me*. New York: Viking.

This book can help young children realize the many different names for houses. For instance, "a husk is a house for a corn ear," "a pod is a place for a pea," and "a teepee's a house for a Cree."

Schwartz, Alvin. 1983. *Unriddling*. New York: Lippincott.

Roam around in this book and you're sure to get hooked. On pages 40–41, Schwartz gives a punctuation riddle to puzzle over, and on pages 48–49, there are letter riddles to figure out. Number 1 riddle says:

> I have seven letters.
> The first two stand for a boy.
> The first three stand for a girl.
> The first four stand for a brave boy.
> But all my letters stand for a brave girl.
> What word am I?

Be sure also to look at Schwartz's *Chin Music: Tall Talk and Other Talk* (1979).

Terban, Marvin. 1982. *Eight Ate: A Feast of Homonym Riddles*. New York: Clarion.

An example of the many riddles that can be found in this paperback is: "How does Moose begin a letter to his cousin? 'Dear Deer . . .' "
It should not take much to get children enticed to fill the classroom with their own homonym riddles. To ensure that you will have word fanatics, expose them to several other Clarion paperbacks like Terban's *In a Pickle and Other Funny Idioms* (1983) and Giulio Maestro's *What's a Frank Frank? Tasty Homograph Riddles* (1984).

Adult Books for Language Enhancement

Blumenfeld, Warren S. 1986. *Jumbo Shrimp and Other Almost Perfect Oxymorons*. New York: Perigee.

In ninety-six pages the author incorporates hundreds of oxymorons such as *faulty logic, extensive briefing, first annual,* and *relative truth*. If you would like to submit oxymorons that Blumenfeld did not include, he invites you to send them to him at P.O. Box 824003, Atlanta, GA 30324.

Brandreth, Gyles. 1980. *The Joy of Lex*. New York: William Morrow.

The subtitle of this book is "How to Have Fun with 860,341,500 Words!" Each chapter begins with a letter of the alphabet (frontwards *and* backwards). In Chapter Two, "Brave New Words," the reader sees some words Shakespeare coined, such as *assassinate, bump, laughable,* and *monumental.* He also coined 1,996 other words! The reader is told how English has gained new words through science, wars, and technology; many examples are listed. On page 52 the term *antigrams* is described. Antigrams are "anagrams with a difference: the new word or words created out of the original word or words have the opposite instead of a similar meaning." One example is "misfortune—it's more fun." Spoonerisms, malapropisms, lipograms, 100 collectives, and much, much more are included in this book. Fifty of the collectives can be found in the dictionary, and the other fifty are ones the author has come across elsewhere, and they are quite funny! Examples are: "a lot of realtors" and "a range of ovens" (279–280).

Editors of the American Heritage Dictionaries. 1986. *Word Mysteries and Histories: From Quiche to Humble Pie.* Boston: Houghton Mifflin.

Language arts teachers will be interested to discover that *glamour* comes from the Greek word *grammatiké*, which originally meant "pertaining to letters or literature" (99). *Legend* is derived from the Latin word *legenda,* a form of the verb *legere,* "to read" (143). We write *Xmas* with an *X* because *X* represents the Greek letter *chi*—the first letter for the Greek form of *Christ* (284).

*Sperling, Susan Kelz. 1981. *Tenderfeet and Ladyfingers*. New York: Viking.

This discusses some one hundred words and phrases that deal with various parts of the human anatomy, arranged from head to toe. Some include: "by the skin of my teeth," "lie through his teeth," and "to lick one's chops." A fascinating book, as are other of Sperling's works, including *Poplollies and Bellibones: A Celebration of Lost Words* (1979, New York: Penguin) and *Murfles and Wink-a-Peeps: Funny Old Words for Kids* (1985, New York: Clarkson N. Potter).

Tompkins, Gail E., and David B. Yaden, Jr. 1986. *Answering Students' Questions about Words.* Urbana, Ill.: National Council of Teachers of English.

This excellent paperback is designed "to provide information, gleaned from the history of the English language, to help elementary and middle school/junior high school teachers answer their students' questions about language. Most of the questions that students ask focus on the seeming lack of consistency in English: irregular plural and past tense forms, silent letters, British and American spelling contrasts, synonyms and homonyms" (1).

Some topics covered in this helpful monograph include: "History of the English Language," "Borrowing and Other Sources of New Words," "English Orthography," "Stabilizing Influences," "Etymologies," "Spelling," and "Forming New Words." The paperback is divided into two sections. The first is concerned with theory and research, while the second part focuses on practice. The practice section contains twenty-three outstanding exercises, called "Extensions," that teachers can use with their pupils. In addition, at the end of *Answering Students' Questions about Words*, there are excellent bibliographies as well as workbooks and activity books.

References

Adelson, Leone. 1972. *Dandelions Don't Bite: The Story of Words.* New York: Pantheon.

Burgess, Gellet. No date. *Burgess Unabridged.* Ann Arbor: Midway Press.

Carew, Jan. 1974. *The Third Gift.* Boston: Little, Brown.

Epstein, Beryl, and Sam Epstein. 1964. *What's Behind the Word?* New York: Scholastic.

Farb, Peter. 1973. *Word Play.* New York: Bantam.

Ferguson, Charles W. 1964. *The Abecedarian Book.* Boston: Little, Brown.

Hubbell, Patricia. 1958. *Catch Me a Wind.* Paterson, N.J.: Atheneum.

Lionni, Leo. 1973. *Frederick.* New York: Knopf/Pantheon.

Lipton, James. 1968. *An Exaltation of Larks.* New York: Grossman.

McCormack, Jo Ann. 1967. *The Story of Our Language.* Columbus, Ohio: Merrill.

Merriam, Eve. 1960. *A Gaggle of Geese.* New York: Knopf.

————. 1965. *Small Fry.* New York: Knopf.

Miller, Albert G. 1974. *Where Did That Word Come From?* Glendale, Calif.: Bowmar.

Newman, Edwin. 1974. *Strictly Speaking.* New York: Bobbs-Merrill.

Ramage, Corinne. 1975. *The Joneses.* Philadelphia: Lippincott.

Parish, Peggy. 1963. *Amelia Bedelia.* New York: Harper.

Severn, Bill. 1966. *People Words.* New York: Ives Washburn.

Sorel, Nancy. 1970. *Word People.* New York: American Heritage.

Sutherland, Zena, and May Hill Arbuthnot. 1986. *Children and Books.* 7th ed. Glenview, Ill.: Scott Foresman.

Tiedt, Iris M., and Sidney W. Tiedt. 1975. *Contemporary English in the Elementary School.* 2d ed. Englewood Cliffs, N.J.: Prentice-Hall.

Warner, Bob. 1975. *The Elephant's Visit.* Boston: Little, Brown.

Related Readings

Blachowicz, Camille L. Z. 1985. Vocabulary Development and Reading: From Research to Instruction. *The Reading Teacher* 38:876–81.

The author points out that the relation between word knowledge and reading performance (i.e., comprehension) is well established, though there are significant differences in points of view about how to enhance word knowledge. She describes two positions: (1) the "instrumentalist position," which suggests that reading comprehension depends on rapid access to word meanings; and (2) the "knowledge position," which is conceptual and emphasizes relational categories. The author concludes by suggesting seven clues from the research on comprehension which she feels guide the way teachers should bring children and words together.

Brooke, Pamela. 1986. Language Is a History Mystery. *Instructor* 96:80–81ff.

The author opens with an amazing assertion: there are more words in English than in any other language! She then goes on to present, in brief fashion, a bit of the history of how English words have come into being, taking in such wordmaking processes as amalgams, blends, assortments, combinations, and conglomerations. For each of these, she gives examples. She describes the geographic mobility of words, tracing from the Indo-European roots through the fifteenth-century voyages of exploration, through the colonists coming to America. At this point, she picks up with the idea of conscious inventing of new words, and gives more examples. The article ends with several classroom activities to involve children in studying the origins of words.

Gaines, Jay. 1987. Business-Word Origins. *American Way,* August 5, 26–27.

In this brief airline magazine piece, the author writes of a variety of words we encounter every day, about whose meanings we seldom think. *Retail,* for example, comes from a very early use by French woodcutters of an even earlier Latin word *talea,* which means "to cut again." They would cut the logs, and then the village dealer would recut them before selling, hence the term. *Broker* is old French (from *brokeor*); *boss* is Dutch, while *stenographer* comes from a Greek word which combines two terms (*stenos,* meaning "narrow or close," and *graphein* meaning "to write"). The article finishes with some references to books about word origins.

Tompkins, Gail E., and Eileen Tway. 1985. Adventuring with Words. *Childhood Education* 61:361–65.

A useful annotated list of children's books about words, helpfully organized into categories like word play and games, riddles, jokes, rhymes and verse, sounds and words, and word histories.

2 Using Picture Books for Reading Vocabulary Development

Alden J. Moe
Lehigh University

In the previous chapter, A. Barbara Pilon gave an enthusiastic overview of vocabulary development and recommended a wide variety of tradebooks that teachers can use to encourage children's interest in words.

In this chapter, Alden J. Moe shares his conviction that picture books can be consciously used to increase children's vocabulary. Children come to school with impressive speaking and listening vocabularies. The school, then, is confronted with the problem of helping children continue to increase their command of words and meanings. After presenting the results of his analysis of vocabulary load in more than 150 books, the author suggests a procedure for their use in a program designed to increase children's vocabulary.

Using picture books to develop and expand a child's reading vocabulary is an excellent way to increase reading achievement. Frequent classroom use of picture books is recommended because the vocabularies of many picture books allow for successful reading while new words are being learned. The techniques presented and the books listed in this chapter may be used at any of the elementary school levels. The focus, however, will be directed at those teachers who are concerned with vocabulary development at the primary levels of reading instruction.

Specifically, this chapter will present (1) a rationale for using picture books, (2) a review of the listening and speaking vocabularies of children, (3) a plan for introducing the new words in a picture book to children, and (4) a listing of picture books with easy vocabularies.

A Rationale for Using Picture Books

The importance of using picture books both in the home and in the school has been emphasized in the widely circulated *Becoming A Nation of Readers* (Anderson et al. 1985). The more exposure children have to printed language prior to their formal schooling and during the early years of reading instruction, the more likely they are to become proficient readers. Picture books not only provide experience with printed language, they also provide a variety of eye-catching, interesting illustrations (Cullinan 1981; Stewig, this volume) which capture a child's attention. An example of these delightful illustrations is found on the facing page.

The child who begins formal reading instruction will probably already have had a variety of prereading literary experiences. Such experiences should include listening to stories read by a parent or teacher and fun with the many good wordless picture books (Larrick 1976; Larrick 1982; Degler 1979). However, children without these previous experiences will benefit also. All children like stories, and reading stories aloud is one of the best means of helping them acquire a match between book language and oral language (Cazden 1981; McCormick 1977; Moe 1975).

While programs published specifically for the teaching of reading may differ and represent varying philosophies of instruction, there is little disagreement today about the use of picture books. They represent a variety of topics and interests, are readily available (or definitely should be!), and are, without question, educationally sound. Picture books should be used in the school and in the home with all children.

Speaking and Listening Vocabularies

Children enter school with extensive speaking and listening vocabularies. By the time children have reached the age of five, their speaking vocabulary has grown to approximately 2,000 words. When children begin grade one, their speaking vocabulary exceeds 4,000 words (Moe, Hopkins, and Rush 1982) and may even approach as many as 15,000 different words (Smith 1941), although it is more likely to be closer to the lower figure (Chall 1987). It also appears that even the most disadvantaged of inner-city children have extensive speaking vocabularies upon entrance to the first grade (Sherk 1973).

Listening vocabularies are even larger. Although research findings vary greatly, it is evident that first graders can listen to and understand between 10,000 and 20,000 different words. Children enter school with a richness in vocabulary; they already "know"—in an understanding sense—more words than they will learn to read in the first five or six years of school.

Reprinted by permission of Four Winds Press, an imprint of Macmillan Publishing Company from THE PURPLE COAT by Amy Hest, illustrated by Amy Schwartz. Illustrations copyright © 1986 Amy Schwartz.

Where does the teacher begin in order to help children with this rich language background match the spoken words they know and written words they do not know? Generally, the teacher begins with some published, packaged program designed specifically for the purpose of teaching children how to read. An alternative approach could be provided, using picture books and other tradebooks as the basic instructional materials (Miller and McKenna 1988), but this is usually not the case.

Picture Books with Easy Vocabularies

For primary-grade children there are many good picture books to choose from (Cianciolo 1981; Cullinan 1981), but selection may become a problem at the beginning levels where the child may possess a reading vocabulary of only a few dozen words. However, with a limited reading vocabulary—a pre-primer vocabulary of forty to fifty words, for example—the child can independently read some trade-books, especially if the books have been read orally by the teacher to the class.

Beginning with books like *Have You Seen My Duckling,* written with only nine different words, or *Drummer Hoff,* with only thirty different words, the books in the list at the end of this chapter provide the framework for a sequential vocabulary development program using picture books. Since most current primers contain about 250 different words, very few books listed here have a greater number of different words than the average primer.

Because of individual tastes, not all children will want to read each book in the list. However, all the books are of high quality and have been selected for their literary merit as well as their vocabularies. Whether they are introduced systematically or incidentally, these books ought to be available for students in the primary grades.

Introducing Unknown Words

Specific book selection and the introduction of new words may be a problem for the teacher, so a step-by-step plan is suggested. The primary-grade teacher has a good idea which words are already a part of the students' reading vocabularies. In selecting a book, the teacher's main concerns are that it contain a minimum of new or difficult words and have understandable and interesting content. Books may be selected from the booklist by the number of different words each book contains.

After the teacher has selected the book, it should be read to identify any new words that may not be part of the students' reading vocabularies. In almost all cases, however, these "new" words will already be part of the students' listening and speaking vocabularies.

An example of how a teacher might identify potentially difficult words may be found in the use of *Today I Thought I'd Run Away* by Jane Johnson. A quick perusal of the book may identify new words, such as *ogre, goblin, demon, mountain,* and *blizzard.* Some discussion of these words prior to the teacher's reading may be appropriate. Students might be told, for example, that *ogres, goblins,* and *demons* are different kinds of monsters, since the word *monster* will be familiar to them.

The next step is for the teacher to read the book orally to the students, paying special attention to the new words. These words may be highlighted by writing them on the chalkboard or, perhaps, by using flashcards prepared in advance. It should be emphasized, however, that the introduction and discussion of new words should not detract interest from the story itself.

While the teacher should introduce new words in the process of sharing the book with the class, it is *not* absolutely essential that all new words be introduced in advance. Often the context in which the word is used—as well as the pictures—will provide the meaning of the word for students.

After the teacher has read the book orally to the class and introduced potentially difficult words, students should immediately be given an opportunity to read the book independently. Through independent reading, students' reading vocabularies will be expanded.

If most of the picture books listed here can be made available to primary-grade children, and if the teacher will introduce these books and their respective new words, the school will have in operation a program that will improve language competencies and reinforce the goals of the reading program.

Recommended Books for Classroom Use

This alphabetical (by author) booklist of selected tradebooks can be used as the basis for a vocabulary development program for primary-grade children. The numeral in parentheses after each title indicates the total number of words contained in the book.

An asterisk (*) before an entry indicates that at the time the revised edition of *Using Literature in the Elementary Classroom* went to press,

that particular title was out of print, according to *Books in Print.*
Those books likely are still available from your local public or school
library.

Adams, Adrienne. 1985. *A Woggle of Witches* (139). New York: Aladdin.

Alexander, Martha. 1969. *The Story Grandmother Told* (147). New
York: Dial.

———. 1976. *I Sure Am Glad to See You, Blackboard Bear* (133). New
York: Dial.

———. 1977. *Blackboard Bear* (64). New York: Dial.

*Allamand, Pascale. 1976. *The Camel Who Left the Zoo* (146). New York:
Scribner's.

*Anglund, Joan. 1963. *Cowboy's Secret Life* (63). New York: Harcourt,
Brace, Jovanovich.

*Asch, Frank. 1976. *Good Lemonade* (126). New York: Franklin Watts.

*Balian, Lorna. 1967. *I Love You, Mary Jane* (79). Nashville: Abingdon.

Barrett, Judith. 1974. *Animals Should Definitely Not Wear Clothing* (65).
New York: Aladdin.

———. 1982. *Cloudy with a Chance of Meatballs* (419). New York:
Aladdin.

Barton, Byron. 1978. *Hester* (128). New York: Puffin.

Bel Geddes, Barbara. 1972. *So Do I* (75). New York: Grosset and
Dunlap.

Beskow, Elsa. 1929. *Pelle's New Suit* (158). New York: Harper and
Row.

*Brandenberg, Franz. 1973. *Fresh Cider and Pie* (104). New York:
Macmillan.

———. 1978. *I Wish I Was Sick, Too* (118). New York: Puffin.

Bright, Robert. 1985. *My Red Umbrella* (68). New York: Morrow
Junior Books.

Brown, Marc. 1986. *Arthur's Nose* (150). Boston: Joy Street Books.

———. 1986. *Arthur's Tooth* (311). Boston: Little, Brown.

Brown, Marcia. 1982. *Once a Mouse* (156). New York: Aladdin.

Brown, Margaret W. 1984. *Good Night Moon* (54). New York: Harper
and Row.

Caple, Kathy. 1986. *The Purse* (272). Boston: Houghton Mifflin.

Carle, Eric. 1981. *The Very Hungry Caterpillar* (107). New York:
Putnam.

Carrick, Carol. 1967. *The Brook* (119). New York: Macmillan.

————. 1988. *What Happened to Patrick's Dinosaurs?* (185). New York: Clarion.

Christelow, Eileen. 1983. *Mr. Murphy's Marvelous Invention* (441). New York: Clarion.

————. 1988. *The Robbery at the Diamond Dog Diner* (390). New York: Clarion.

Cleary, Beverly. 1987. *Two Dog Biscuits* (254). New York: Dell.

Cohen, Miriam. 1986. *Jim's Dog Muffins* (232). New York: Dell.

————. 1987. *Liar, Liar, Pants on Fire!* (280). New York: Dell.

————. 1987. *Starring First Grade* (249). New York: Dell.

Cooney, Barbara. 1985. *Miss Rumphius* (418). New York: Puffin.

Cuyler, Margery. 1986. *Freckles and Willie: A Valentine's Day Story* (278). New York: Holt, Rinehart and Winston.

*Delton, Judy. 1982. *The Goose Who Wrote a Book* (341). Minneapolis: Carolrhoda Books.

*Demuth, Patricia Brennan. 1986. *Max, the Bad-Talking Parrot* (513). New York: Dodd, Mead.

De Paola, Tomie, and Arnold Lobel. 1981. *The Comic Adventures of Old Mother Hubbard and Her Dog* (91). New York: Harcourt, Brace, Jovanovich.

*deRegniers, Beatrice Schenk. 1956. *Was It a Good Trade?* (77). New York: Harcourt, Brace, Jovanovich.

————. 1974. *May I Bring a Friend?* (151). New York: Aladdin.

Devlin, Wende, and Harry Devlin. 1986. *Cranberry Valentine* (334). New York: Four Winds Press.

Emberley, Barbara A. 1967. *Drummer Hoff* (30). Englewood Cliffs, N.J.: Prentice-Hall.

Freeman, Don. 1978. *A Rainbow of My Own* (138). New York: Puffin.

Geringer, Laura. 1987. *A Three Hat Day* (340). New York: Trophy.

Ginsburg, Mirra. 1988. *The Chick and the Duckling* (32). New York: Aladdin.

Goffstein, M. B. 1976. *Fish for Supper* (106). New York: Dial.

*Greaves, Margaret. 1985. *Once There Were No Pandas* (388). New York: E. P. Dutton.

*Greenberg, Dolly. 1968. *Oh Lord, I Wish I Was a Buzzard* (105). New York: Macmillan.

Hallinan, P. K. 1973. *We're Very Good Friends, My Brother and I* (137). Chicago: Children's Press.

Havill, Juanita. 1985. *Jamaica's Find* (274). Boston: Houghton Mifflin.

Hest, Amy. 1986. *The Purple Coat* (553). New York: Four Winds Press.

Hogrogian, Nonny. 1974. *One Fine Day* (150). New York: Aladdin.

Holl, Adelaide. 1965. *The Rain Puddle* (155). New York: Lothrop, Lee and Shepard.

*Hutchins, Pat. 1970. *Clocks and More Clocks* (92). New York: Macmillan.

———. 1971. *Rosie's Walk* (25). New York: Aladdin.

———. 1971. *Titch* (46). New York: Macmillan.

———. 1972. *Good-Night, Owl* (51). New York: Macmillan.

———. 1974. *The Wind Blew* (91). New York: Macmillan.

———. 1976. *Don't Forget the Bacon!* (31). New York: Greenwillow Books.

———. 1986. *The Surprise Party* (103). New York: Macmillan.

———. 1988. *The Very Worst Monster* (129). New York: Mulberry Books.

Jensen, Virginia Allen. 1977. *Sara and the Door* (93). Reading, Mass.: Addison-Wesley.

Johnson, Jane. 1986. *Today I Thought I'd Run Away* (115). New York: E. P. Dutton.

Keats, Ezra. 1962. *The Snowy Day* (157). New York: Viking.

———. 1983. *Peter's Chair* (153). New York: Trophy.

———. 1987. *Goggles* (149). New York: Aladdin.

Kellogg, Steven. 1977. *The Mystery of the Missing Red Mitten* (128). New York: Dial.

———. 1985. *Chicken Little* (292). New York: William Morrow.

Kent, Jack. 1985. *Joey Runs Away* (202). Englewood Cliffs, N.J.: Prentice-Hall.

*Krasilovsky, Phyllis. 1962. *The Very Little Boy* (103). New York: Doubleday.

Kraus, Robert. 1972. *Milton, the Early Riser* (81). New York: E. P. Dutton.

———. 1972. *Whose Mouse Are You?* (57). New York: Aladdin.

*———. 1974. *Herman the Helper* (48). New York: E. P. Dutton.

———. 1986. *Where Are You Going, Little Mouse* (70). New York: Greenwillow Books.

———. 1987. *Leo, the Late Bloomer* (78). Reissued ed. New York: Crowell Junior Books.

———. 1987. *Owliver* (74). Englewood Cliffs, N.J.: Prentice-Hall.

Krauss, Ruth. 1945. *The Carrot Seed* (45). New York: Harper and Row.

——. 1947. *The Growing Story* (158). New York: Harper and Row.

Kunhardt, Edith. 1986. *Danny's Birthday* (146). New York: Greenwillow Books.

*Langner, Nora. 1969. *Miss Lucy* (50). New York: Macmillan.

Langstaff, John. 1974. *Oh, A-Hunting We Will Go* (45). New York: Atheneum.

*Lapp, Eleanor J. 1976. *The Mice Came in Early This Year* (117). Chicago: A. Whitman.

Lenski, Lois. 1980. *The Little Farm* (98). New York: McKay.

*Lent, Blair. 1968. *Why the Sun and the Moon Live in the Sky* (147). Boston: Houghton Mifflin.

Lester, Alison. 1985. *Clive Eats Alligators* (132). Boston: Houghton Mifflin.

McPhail, David. 1988. *The Bear's Toothache* (111). Boston: Little, Brown.

McQueen, John Troy. 1986. *A World Full of Monsters* (91). New York: Crowell.

Margolin, Harriet. 1985. *Busy Bear's Cupboard* (39). New York: Putnam.

Marshall, James. 1973. *Yummers!* (259). Boston: Houghton Mifflin.

——. 1974. *George & Martha* (223). Boston: Houghton Mifflin.

Martin, Rafe, and Ed Young. 1985. *Foolish Rabbit's Big Mistake* (394). New York: Putnam.

Mayer, Mercer. 1980. *You're the Scaredy-Cat* (120). New York: Four Winds Press. (Reprint of 1974 edition by Parents' Magazine Press.)

——. 1987. *There's an Alligator under My Bed* (115). New York: Dial.

*Mendoza, George. 1968. *The Gillygoofang* (102). New York: Dial.

*Miles, Miska. 1976. *Chicken Forgets* (145). Boston: Little, Brown.

Montaufier, Poupa. 1985. *One Summer at Grandmother's House* (1,138). Minneapolis: Carolrhoda Books.

Murphy, Jill. 1986. *Five Minutes' Peace* (196). New York: Putnam.

Nodset, Joan. 1963. *Go Away, Dog* (83). New York: Harper and Row.

——. 1973. *Come Here, Cat* (84). New York: Harper and Row.

Numeroff, Laura Joffe. 1985. *If You Give a Mouse a Cookie* (122). New York: Harper and Row.

Pinkwater, Daniel. 1984. *Bear's Picture* (129). New York: E. P. Dutton.

*Pinkwater, Manus. 1976. *Around Fred's Bed* (59). Englewood Cliffs, N.J.: Prentice-Hall.

Pryor, Bonnie. 1985. *Grandpa Bear* (352). New York: William Morrow.

Raskin, Ellen. 1977. *Nothing Ever Happens on My Block* (80). New York: Aladdin.

Rice, Eve. 1983. *What Sadie Sang* (105). New York: Greenwillow Books.

*Rockwell, Anne. 1973. *The Awful Mess* (111). New York: Parents' Magazine Press.

*Ross, Jessica. 1972. *Fanona the Beautiful* (152). New York: Holt, Rinehart and Winston.

*Rossetti, Christina. 1971. *What Is Pink?* (45). New York: Macmillan.

Ryan, Cheli Durán, and Arnold Lobel. 1986. *Hildilid's Night* (187). New York: Macmillan.

Schumacher, Claire. 1985. *King of the Zoo* (209). New York: William Morrow.

Sendak, Maurice. 1988. *Where the Wild Things Are* (139). New York: Trophy.

Sharmat, Marjorie W. 1985. *Attila the Angry* (441). New York: Holiday House.

Shulevitz, Uri. 1988. *Rain Rain Rivers* (95). New York: Sunburst.

Stanek, Muriel. 1985. *All Alone after School* (421). Chicago: A. Whitman.

Steptoe, John. 1984. *The Story of Jumping Mouse* (468). New York: Lothrop, Lee and Shepard.

Tafuri, Nancy. 1986. *Have You Seen My Duckling?* (9). New York: Puffin.

Turkle, Brinton. 1985. *Do Not Open* (407). New York: E. P. Dutton.

Turner, Ann. 1985. *Dakota Dugout* (242). New York: Macmillan.

Udry, Janice. 1988. *Let's Be Enemies* (112). New York: Trophy.

Wells, Rosemary. 1978. *Morris's Disappearing Bag: A Christmas Story* (158). New York: Dial.

———. 1980. *Noisy Nora* (103). New York: Dial.

———. 1986. *Max's Christmas* (95). New York: Dial.

*Williams, Barbara. 1976. *Someday, Said Mitchell* (119). New York: E.P. Dutton.

*Williams, Garth. 1970. *The Chicken Book* (56). New York: Delacorte.

Williams, Linda. 1988. *The Little Old Lady Who Was Not Afraid of Anything* (185). New York: Trophy.

Wooding, Sharon L. 1986. *Arthur's Christmas Wish* (524). New York: Atheneum.

Yolen, Jane. 1978. *No Bath Tonight* (300). New York: Crowell.

Yorinks, Arthur. 1986. *Hey, Al* (268). New York: Farrar, Straus, and Giroux.

Ziefert, Harriet, and Carol Nickalus. 1986. *Good Night, Lewis!* (220). New York: Random House.

Zolotow, Charlotte. 1958. *Do You Know What I'll Do?* (93). New York: Harper and Row.

———. 1987. *May I Visit?* (143). New York: Harper and Row.

References

Anderson, Richard C., Elfrieda H. Hiebert, Judith A. Scott, and Ian Wilkinson. 1985. *Becoming a Nation of Readers: The Report of the Commission on Reading.* Washington, D.C.: The National Institute of Education.

Cazden, Courtney B. 1981. *Language in Early Childhood Education.* 2d ed. Washington, D.C.: National Association for the Education of Young Children.

Chall, Jeanne S. 1987. Two Vocabularies for Reading: Recognition and Meaning. In *The Nature of Vocabulary Acquisition,* edited by Margaret G. McKeown and Mary E. Curtis. Hillsdale, N.J.: Erlbaum.

Cianciolo, Patricia, editor. 1981. *Picture Books for Children.* 2d ed. Chicago: American Library Association.

Cullinan, Bernice E. 1981. *Literature and the Child.* New York: Harcourt, Brace, Jovanovich.

Degler, Lois. 1979. Putting Words into Wordless Picture Books. *The Reading Teacher* 32:399–402.

Larrick, Nancy. 1976. Wordless Picture Books and the Teaching of Reading. *The Reading Teacher* 29:743–46.

———. 1982. *A Parent's Guide to Children's Reading.* 5th ed. Philadelphia: Westminster Press.

McCormick, Sandra. 1977. Should You Read Aloud to Your Children? *Language Arts* 54:139–43, 163.

Miller, John W., and Michael C. McKenna. 1988. *Teaching Reading in the Elementary Classroom.* Scottsdale, Ariz.: Gorsuch Scarisbrick Publishers.

Moe, Alden J. 1975. Using the Child's Oral Language in Beginning Reading Instruction. *Reading Horizons* 116:32–35.

Moe, Alden J., Carol J. Hopkins, and R. Timothy Rush. 1982. *The Vocabulary of First Grade Children.* Springfield, Ill.: Charles C. Thomas Publishing.

Sherk, John K. 1973. *A Word-Count of Spoken English of Culturally Disadvantaged Preschool and Elementary Students.* Kansas City: University of Missouri at Kansas City.

Smith, M. K. 1941. Measurement of the Size of General English Vocabulary through the Elementary Grades and High School. *Genetic Psychology Monographs* 24:311–45.

Teale, William H. 1984. Reading to Young Children: Its Significance for Literacy Development. In *Awakening to Literacy,* edited by H. Goelman, A. A. Oberg, and F. Smith. Exeter, N.H.: Heinemann Educational Books.

Related Readings

Baumann, James F., and Dale D. Johnson, editors. 1984. *Reading Instruction and the Beginning Teacher: A Practical Guide.* Minneapolis: Burgess.

Despite the title, this is also an excellent source of information for experienced teachers. The first three chapters provide strategies for vocabulary instruction. The book also contains several excellent chapters on using tradebooks in the classroom. These chapters are highly recommended to those who feel that they are "bound" to or by basal readers.

Edgar, Dale, Joseph O'Rourke, and Walter B. Barbe. 1986. *Vocabulary Building: A Process Approach.* Columbus, Ohio: Zaner-Bloser.

This comprehensive volume is especially good for upper elementary and junior high students. Many sample lessons are included for teacher use. Separate chapters on using word games and methods of testing vocabulary make this an excellent reference.

Johnson, Dale D., and P. David Pearson. 1984. *Teaching Reading Vocabulary.* 2d ed. New York: Holt, Rinehart and Winston.

This paperback book provides many sample lessons and suggested activities in most areas of reading vocabulary instruction. It is one of the most widely used sources of instructional techniques available.

Johnson, Dale D., and Alden J. Moe. 1983. *The Ginn Word Book for Teachers: A Basic Lexicon.* Boston: Ginn.

This source provides a list of the words the authors believe should be taught in elementary school reading and language arts instruction. Separate lists are provided for grades one, two, and three. A unique feature of this "word book" is that one major source from which the lexicon was derived was a corpus of words based on over 300 widely used picture books.

Kimmel, Margaret Mary, and Elizabeth Segel. 1984. *For Reading Out Loud!* New York: Dell.

As the publisher indicates, this book is essentially "a guide to sharing books with children." It is filled with activities concerning books. It also contains information on how to read aloud and how to introduce books. This volume also contains short summaries of some of the more popular tradebooks, plus extensive listings of good books by grade or age level.

3 The Tradebook as an Instructional Tool: Strategies in Approaching Literature

Helen Felsenthal
University of Pennsylvania

Knowing individual words does not ensure reading proficiency. Readers must be able to sense the interrelationship of words and respond to the total message the author has created, whether that be a sentence, a paragraph, or an entire literary unit. In this chapter, Helen Felsenthal describes ways to help children approach literature, using works of literature as a major instructional tool for teaching foundational reading skills. Felsenthal describes a specific approach to literary genres through understanding basic elements of a genre and through use of self-questioning techniques. To help children learn about literature, Felsenthal plans experiences with character, plot, and setting, exposing students to literature that treats these elements in different ways. Children are taught metacognitive strategies on how to ask themselves questions about the author's use of these elements. The final goal of such reading and self-questioning is heightened awareness of genre and the author's intent, as well as a deeper understanding of what was read.

In the hierarchy of reading skills, the ability to read critically is considered the highest level of reading. Although many components of critical reading can be taught through exercises and worksheets, the use of children's books in their entirety provides an ideal opportunity to develop critical reading while enhancing both reading skill and enjoyment. Literature comes in many forms, and different skills are needed for understanding the various genres or types of literature.

This chapter presents approaches to the teaching of basic reading skills that are conducive to the understanding and enjoyment of two literary forms: fiction and nonfiction. Four types of fiction are addressed: realistic, fanciful, historical, and biographical. Two types of nonfiction are considered: exposition and argument. The teaching method is centered around literary works as the major instructional tool and offers self-questioning strategies for understanding each genre.

Recent research supports the self-questioning process as a form of metacognition valuable in developing comprehension skills, since understanding is reached through the ability to monitor and regulate one's own cognitive processes (Gaskins and Baron 1985). Metacognition has been called "learning to learn." Brown (1985) states that metacognition is composed of two elements: (1) knowledge about cognition and (2) regulation of cognition. The first is "knowledge that readers have about their own cognitive resources and the compatibility between themselves as readers and the demands of a variety of reading situations" (Brown 1985, 501). The second form of metacognition focuses on the self-regulating, or cognitive monitoring, mechanisms used by active learners during an attempt to solve problems. These mechanisms can take various forms such as checking, planning, evaluating, testing, revising, and remediating (Baker and Brown 1984).

This chapter focuses on the metacognitive process of self-questioning, with the goal of having readers apply the questioning process automatically so that the strategy becomes a natural way to approach literature. Teachers commonly use questions in developing comprehension, and there is a large body of research on the effectiveness of using adjunct questions or within-text questions (Anderson and Brown 1975). The major difference between the use of adjunct questions and the self-questioning process is that in the former, questions are provided for the students. In self-questioning, students generate their own questions, developing the continuous process of hypothesis generation. Two types of hypotheses are generated: interpretations and predictions. Interpretations involve hypotheses about what is happening now; predictions are hypotheses about what will happen next.

The advantage of using a metacognitive approach is that students learn both the basic elements of a genre and the important questions to ask as they read each genre. This questioning process is continuous so that the strategy becomes a natural way to guide the reading of literature. As students become more advanced readers, their application of the basic strategy becomes more sophisticated, enhancing understanding and enjoyment.

Learning about Fiction

Children are introduced to fiction in their early years, and they encounter it frequently throughout the elementary school years.

Reading fiction for recreational purposes can provide a lifelong source of entertainment and information.

Basic Elements of Fiction

Most fiction contains three basic elements: character (who the story is about), action or plot (what happened), and setting (where and when does it happen). Figure 1† summarizes the basic elements in fiction, describes kinds of fiction, and indicates the important questions to ask when reading fiction.

To initiate a lesson, students can be asked to give examples of these elements in a favorite fiction story. They can name some characters, tell about the action or plot, and describe the setting, speculating upon which of the elements in their favorite stories are not real. From this description, fiction can be defined as storytelling in which at least one of the above three elements is made up by the author. For example, after reading *In the Year of the Boar and Jackie Robinson* by Betty Bao Lord (1986; New York: Trophy), children might be asked to think about such questions as:

Definition: The three basic elements in fiction are:
> *1. Character*
> *2. Action*
> *3. Setting*

Fiction is writing in which one or more of the three elements are made up, not true.

Kinds of Fiction:

1. *Realistic fiction:* The story could possibly happen, but parts are made up by the author for the story.
   a. *Historical fiction:* A real setting in the past.
   b. *Biographical fiction:* The main character must be real.
2. *Fanciful fiction:* Character, action, or setting are unlikely or impossible.

Questions to Ask as You Read:

1. *Character:* Who is it about?
2. *Action:* What happens? What is the problem?
3. *Setting:* Where and when does it happen?

Figure 1. Learning about Fiction

---

† The author grants permission to reproduce the figures of worksheets in this chapter as wall charts or individual student guides.

1. Was Shirley Temple Wong a real or made-up character?
2. What things about her make you feel that way?
3. Is Brooklyn an actual city?
4. What information leads you to this conclusion?
5. Could the events described in the story actually take place?
6. If you aren't certain if the events really happened, how could you find out?

In this example, the character and most of the action was probably made up by the author, but the setting (Brooklyn) is a real city.

Basic Questions about Fiction

The answers derived from basic questions about fiction help students understand and remember the story and help them identify the kind of fiction they are reading.

Ask children to consider questions about the *character* such as: Who is the main character? Is it someone who really lived, could likely exist, or was made up for the story? Who are the other characters? Are they real or made up, likely or unlikely to exist? What do the characters' speech, action, ideas, or appearance tell you about them? What reasons do the characters have for the things they do? How do the characters feel about each other? Do any characters learn something important in the story? Do they change their attitudes or behavior?

Children also need to think about questions related to the *action* in the story. Typical questions could include: Is the main action of the story something that actually happens or something that takes place in the author's imagination? Is the main action something that would be likely to happen or is it made up for the story? What effect does the action have on the characters? What is the primary problem that the characters have? How is the problem solved?

Finally, we want children to discuss questions about the third element of fiction, the *setting*. Questions could include: Where does the action happen? What details tell you that? Is it a real place or a place made up for the story? Is it a likely place? Does the setting indicate a particular period in history? Could the same story happen in a different setting? Why or why not?

Applying the Questions to a Specific Book

A sample application of this technique is used with the book *Dear Mr. Henshaw*, the 1984 Newberry Medal winner by Beverly Cleary

(1988; New York: Scholastic). This realistic fiction is about a ten-year-old boy, Leigh Botts, who develops a letter-writing relationship with Boyd Henshaw, an author of children's books. Leigh is new to his school and is lonely because his mother and father are divorced; Leigh doesn't often see or hear from his father. Mr. Fridley, the school custodian, befriends Leigh, and Leigh gradually makes other friends. The story is told through Leigh's letters to Boyd Henshaw and through the writings in Leigh's diary.

The following is an example of how the questions about character, action, and setting can be applied to this specific story, with possible responses.

Character

1. Who is the main character? Is it someone who actually lived, could likely exist, or was made up for the story?

   Possible response: The main character is Leigh Botts, a ten-year-old sixth grader. He probably is a character made up for the story, but Leigh could have been a real person because he is described as and acts like a real person.

2. Who are the other characters? Are they real or made up, likely or unlikely to exist?

   Possible response: The other characters are Leigh's mother and father; the school custodian, Mr. Fridley; and Leigh's friend, Barry. They are probably made up by the author, but could have lived.

3. What do the characters' speech, action, ideas, or appearance tell you about them?

   Possible response: Through discussion of each character, it can be concluded that the characters fit the plot of the story and play their roles in showing how Leigh struggles for happiness. For example, Leigh's mother tries to help him accept his father's absence. Mr. Fridley helps Leigh to adjust to a new school.

4. What reasons do the characters have for the things they do? How do the characters feel about each other?

   Possible response: Leigh expresses his feelings of anger and loneliness, and his mother and Mr. Fridley try to help him understand his feelings.

5. Do any characters learn something important in the story?

   Possible response: Leigh learns he cannot change some things, such as having his father return home.

Illustration from the title page of DEAR MR. HENSHAW, text by Beverly Cleary, illustrated by Paul O. Zelinsky. Illustration: Copyright © 1983 by Paul O. Zelinsky. By permission of William Morrow and Co., Inc.

6. Do the characters change their attitudes or behavior?

    Possible response: Leigh's father does not change, but Leigh learns how to adjust to his new life.

Action

Although action will have been discussed in relationship to the characters, specific aspects of the action need attention, as illustrated in the following discussion.

7. Is the main action of the story something that actually happens or something that takes place in the author's imagination?

    Possible response: The main action of the story is told in Leigh's letters and diary rather than actually as it happens. Leigh's writing tells about his feelings, but much of the writing describes events with others, such as when Leigh's father comes to visit him.

8. Is the main action something that would be likely to happen or is it made up for the story?

    Possible response: The main action probably was made up for the story and did not really happen, but the story could have happened. For example, the author depicts the difficult financial situation that divorce can cause by describing the family's humble living arrangement and Leigh's being alone more often because his mother must work full-time.

9. What is the main problem that the characters have?

    Possible response: The main problem is Leigh's adjustment to changes in his life, such as the recent divorce of his parents, living in a new place alone with his mother, and going to a new school.

10. How is the problem solved?

    Possible response: The problem gradually lessens as Leigh begins to understand why his parents divorced. Leigh learns how to make new friends through the help of Mr. Fridley and through writing about his problems.

Setting

11. Setting can be discussed in terms of place and time. For example, where does the action happen?

    Possible response: Most of the action takes place in Leigh's head since the book is in letter and diary form. Leigh describes his home, school, and neighborhood.

12. What details tell you that?

   Possible response: The setting is thoroughly described in Leigh's writing, and there are many illustrations of his home and school. Leigh lives in a very small house in a somewhat run-down neighborhood.

13. Is it a real place? A place made up for the story? A likely place?

   Possible response: The setting, although made up for the story, includes likely places such as a school and neighborhood.

14. When does the story take place? Could the same story happen in a different setting? Why or why not?

   Possible response: The setting is contemporary, and most of the story deals with problems common to current times (such as the effects of divorce on family life). The story could happen at a different time, but the setting (home, school) likely would be the same.

Four Types of Fiction

As students look for answers to these basic questions, they can begin to identify the different types of fiction. Most fiction for children can be classified into one of four categories: realistic, fanciful, historical, or biographical. Of these, the first two types are the most common and easily enjoyed.

The reading of fiction serves many functions. Most children read *realistic fiction* for enjoyment, but in the process they can gain insights into their own problems or develop an understanding of others who might be different from them by virtue of race, gender, geographical location, or disability. *Fanciful fiction* encourages the development of imagination and creativity. *Historical fiction* gives meaning to names and dates, and *biographical fiction* provides important role models.

The basic elements of each type of fiction are outlined here:

1. Realistic fiction
   a. uses one or more elements that are made up for the story
   b. uses elements that seem likely
   c. can take place in the past, the present, or the future
2. Fanciful fiction
   a. uses one or more elements that are made up for the story
   b. one or more elements seem unlikely or impossible†

---

† A fine critical analysis of this type of fiction is included in *The Green and Burning Tree* by Eleanor Cameron (1969; Boston: Little, Brown). The book, a collection of essays, features a section on fantasy (pp. 3–136). Cameron speaks with authority on this topic, since she is recognized as one of the most significant writers of fantasy for children.

3. Historical fiction
   a. uses a real time setting in the past
   b. uses elements that are likely
4. Biographical fiction
   a. uses a main character who really lived
   b. uses elements that seem likely

Approaching fiction by identifying the basic elements (character, action, setting) and answering basic questions helps the reader to anticipate what may happen as the story develops. Such attempts to predict plot lead to greater understanding and appreciation of literary fiction.

Learning about Nonfiction

As students progress through school, they encounter nonfiction works more frequently as they begin to read biographies, use reference books, read newspapers, and do independent study in content areas such as science and social studies. Students can learn how to identify different kinds of nonfiction and to answer basic questions during their reading, developing a strategy for reading nonfiction. Figure 2 outlines two kinds of nonfiction and suggests the pertinent questions to pose when reading nonfiction.

Basic Kinds of Nonfiction

There are two main types of nonfiction: exposition and argument. The author's purpose differentiates the two types. Exposition is nonfiction that tries to explain something to the reader or tries to help the reader understand a subject or idea. The second type of nonfiction, argument, tries to persuade the reader or tries to make someone do or believe a certain thing.

Students can be asked to decide the purpose of common types of nonfiction, such as the following:

1. a newspaper editorial asking you to vote for a certain candidate (argument)
2. a book chapter or section that describes the different parts of a flower (exposition)
3. a newspaper article telling how to change a car tire (exposition)
4. a letter asking you to send money to help handicapped children (argument)

Definition: Nonfiction is writing that tells about actual people, events, and things.

Two Main Kinds of Nonfiction:

1. *Exposition*
   a. Tries to explain something
   b. Tries to help the reader understand
   c. Examples of exposition are: (1) books about things or places (news articles, textbooks, encyclopedia articles), (2) biography (the life story of an actual person, told by someone else), (3) autobiography (the life story of an actual person told by that person)
2. *Argument*
   a. Tries to persuade the reader to do or believe something
   b. Tries to make the reader agree with a certain idea
   c. Examples of argument are: (1) editorials, (2) advertisements, (3) letters asking you to help someone or to buy something

Questions to Ask as You Read:

1. What is the subject?
2. What is the main idea?
3. What facts are used? What opinions?
4. What causes are there? What effects?
5. What conclusions are made?
6. What generalizations are used?
7. What ambiguities need to be understood?
8. What is the author's purpose in writing the selection?
9. What kind of nonfiction is this?

Figure 2. Learning about Nonfiction

5. an article that tells why the author likes bird-watching (exposition)

6. a letter asking you to join the Junior Wilderness Society and work to save America's forests from destruction (argument)

7. a biography—the life of an actual person, told by someone else (exposition)

Students can also volunteer other examples of nonfiction and decide whether they are exposition or argument.

Basic Questions about Nonfiction

Answering the following basic questions during the reading of nonfiction can help readers remember the writing and understand the author's purpose. Answers to these questions will help to identify the type of nonfiction. However, not all questions are always appropriate for all nonfiction writing. Typical questions include the following:

1. What is the subject or main theme of the selection?
2. What point of view does the author take in presenting the subject or theme?
3. What facts/opinions are used?
4. What causes are explained?
5. What are the effects of the causes?
6. What conclusions are made?
7. What generalizations are used?
8. What ambiguities need to be understood?
9. What is the author's purpose in writing the selection?

These questions outline the major skills in the development of comprehension. These skills are repeatedly addressed in the teaching of reading, beginning with "picture" reading in kindergarten and continuing throughout formal reading instruction. Many sources are available on ways to teach these skills. Specific techniques are included in the teacher's guides accompanying basal readers. Publishers also offer supplementary materials in the form of kits, worksheets, or exercises. Comprehension is a major area of reading research, with journals and books offering numerous selections on the teaching of comprehension skills (see Orasanu 1986; Pearson 1984; Santa and Hayes 1981; and Singer and Raddell 1985).

Applying the Questions to a Specific Book

Thinking Big by Susan Kuklin (1986; New York: Lothrop, Lee and Shepard) is a nonfiction book about Jaime Osborn, an eight-year-old who is a dwarf. The story explains dwarfism and illustrates how Jaime's life is both similar to and different from her peers. The author's photographs supplement the text and depict Jaime with her family and friends. The book can illustrate the use of questions pertinent to understanding nonfiction.

1. What is the subject or main theme of the book?
    Possible response: The subject of the book is eight-year-old Jaime Osborn, who is a dwarf. The main theme is that dwarfs have lives that are like those of their friends, but because dwarfs are so small, they may have special problems.

Photograph from THINKING BIG by Susan Kuklin. Text: Copyright ©
1986 by Susan Kuklin. Illustrations: Copyright © 1986 by Susan Kuklin.
By permission of Lothrop, Lee and Shepard, a division of William Morrow
and Co., Inc.

2. What point of view does the author take in presenting the
   subject or theme?

   Possible response: Through the use of photographs and
   descriptions of the characteristics of dwarfs, the author tries to
   show that a dwarf can live a normal life and do most things
   that other children can do.

3. What facts/opinions are used?

   Possible response: The author uses facts to explain what
   causes dwarfism and what are the most common physical characteristics. For example, "a dwarf like Jaime has short arms and
   legs on an average body," (1), and "Dwarfs are double jointed"
   (24).

4. What causes are explained and what are the effects of the
   causes?

   Possible response: Some people are uncomfortable with
   someone who is different. The author tells how some other
   children have treated Jaime. "The kindergartners can be nasty,"
   Jaime recalls. "They may call me names like 'look at that little
   baby'..." (20).

5. What conclusions are drawn and what generalizations are used?
   Possible response: The author tries to show that dwarfs are like other people. ("I am like everybody else, just little.")

6. What ambiguities need to be understood?
   Possible response: A person's response to a dwarf can be positive or negative, and a dwarf must learn to deal with different reactions.

7. What is the author's purpose in writing the book?
   Possible response: The author tells the story of the life of a dwarf and shows how her life with family and friends is like other children's lives, yet is different because of the adjustments that must be made because of Jaime's small size.

Summary

Teachers who use tradebooks as instructional tools can choose from a wide range of books, matching the interests and abilities of students with specific literature. Reading strategies for approaching fiction and nonfiction can be developed into several types of lessons. The lesson can take various forms, such as small-group discussions, games, card questions, or forms of creative drama.

A chart or guide outlining the important aspects of each genre can serve as a reference, since repeated practice of the self-questioning strategy is necessary before the technique becomes a natural way to approach literature. A similar student guide for each genre can be given to each pupil to use only as a reference (see Figures 1 and 2). The guides should *not* be used as a worksheet and completed for each book read. Rather, they should be used as reminders of the basic elements of the genre.

The self-questioning approach provides a structure or framework that will help the reader to organize and understand the information presented in print. This metacognitive approach differs from the "skills in isolation" approach where specific skills are taught separately, often without application in actual reading. The reading of fiction and nonfiction requires combinations of reading skills. The understanding of the interrelationships among these skills offers a challenge that students are able to meet if they know the basic structure of each genre. The tradebook can become an exciting and useful instructional tool in the teaching of language skills.

Recommended Books for Classroom Use

Any booklist is essentially arbitrary, and the reader is encouraged to
use books that are appropriate and enjoyable to a particular age
group. The books in these annotated lists were chosen because of
their quality and appeal to various age levels. The topical list represents
both older and more recently published books addressing a variety
of topics.

An asterisk (*) before an entry indicates that at the time the revised
edition of *Using Literature in the Elementary Classroom* went to press,
that particular title was out of print, according to *Books in Print*.
Those books likely are still available from your local public or school
library.

Realistic Fiction

De Paola, Tomie. 1978. *Pancakes for Breakfast.* New York: Harcourt.

In this wordless picture book, children can tell a story by looking
at the pictures. In the story, a woman awakens and decides to make
pancakes, but after collecting eggs from the henhouse and milking
the cow, she decides she has no maple syrup. After returning home
with the syrup, she finds her dog and cat have knocked over the
batter. But she smells her neighbors' pancakes and joins them for
breakfast.

*Fanshawe, Elizabeth. 1975. *Rachel.* New York: Bradbury.

Rachel is a young child who must use a wheelchair. She is main-
streamed in school, has many friends, and learns how to adeptly
maneuver her wheelchair.

Hamilton, Virginia. 1983. *Willie Bea and the Time the Martians Landed.*
New York: Greenwillow Books.

In this story for older children, the author creates a memorable
heroine, Sheema, who is intellectually limited, short, and fat.

Phang, Ruth, and Susan L. Roth. 1984. *Patchwork Tales.* New York:
Atheneum.

A little girl hears bedtime stories from her grandmother concerning
patchwork quilts. Each piece of cloth in the quilt has a history, and
the girl learns about her family through the stories about where the
cloths came from and who owned them.

Steptoe, John. 1983. *Daddy Is a Monster . . . Sometimes.* New York: Trophy.

For young readers, this story and its illustrations show the varied relationship between two black sons and their father. The illustrations show two different reactions to identical incidents while showing a strong father-son relationship.

Williams, Vera B. 1987. *Something Special for Me.* New York: Mulberry.

In this picture storybook, Rosa, the little girl who tells the story, describes how she is to use a coin saved by her mother and grandmother to buy a special birthday gift for herself. Rosa keeps changing her mind about what she wants, but finally buys a used accordion so she can learn to play like her grandmother.

Fanciful Fiction

Corrin, Sara, and Stephen Corrin, editors. 1981. *The Faber Book of Modern Fairy Tales.* Winchester, Mass.: Faber and Faber.

This is a collection of fifteen original fairytale stories written by prominent authors during the last century. These stories could be compared and contrasted with traditional fairytales, focusing on literary elements of the genre, like repetition and flat characters, among others. In this process, students can understand how authors take literary devices and use them for their own purposes.

Goble, Paul. 1986. *The Girl Who Loved Wild Horses.* New York: Aladdin.

A 1979 Caldecott Medal award-winner, this is a folk story of a young Native American girl who becomes so close to the wild horses she loves that she finally becomes one of them.

Mahy, Margaret. 1984. *The Haunting.* New York: Apple.

This tells the adventures of a young boy who has inherited extrasensory perception and finds a similarly gifted great-uncle.

McCully, Emily Arnold. 1984. *Picnic.* New York: Harper.

This is a simple wordless picture book from which a preschooler could create a story aloud. A family of mice loses one of its children off a truck as they head for a picnic. The lost child is finally found and the family settles down for a picnic lunch.

Yolen, Jane. 1984. *Dragon's Blood.* New York: Dell.

Bond servant Jakkin steals a dragon that he trains as a fighter to earn the price of his freedom.

Historical Fiction

Gray, Genevieve. 1978. *How Far, Felipe?* New York: Harper.

This easy-to-read book, set in 1775–1776, tells of families who left Culiacan, Mexico, in 1775 to settle in California under the leadership of Colonel Juan Bautista de Anza. It is an accurate portrayal of the historical setting and the hardships endured by the settlers.

Leech, Jay, and Zane Spencer. 1979. *Bright Fawn and Me.* New York: Crowell.

Written for the young reader and set a century ago, this book describes how a Cheyenne child takes care of her younger sister while the family takes part in an intertribal fair.

Magorian, Michelle. 1986. *Good Night, Mr. Tom.* New York: Trophy.

Set in a small English village during World War II, a child evacuated from London learns to love his caretaker.

Uchida, Yoshiko. 1985. *A Jar of Dreams.* New York: Aladdin.

Eleven-year-old Rinko is embarrassed by her Japanese heritage and describes the prejudice against Japanese-Americans in this Depression era story. Rinko's aunt helps her cope with these problems.

Voigt, Cynthia. 1983. *The Callender Papers.* New York: Atheneum.

An orphaned girl sorts through papers from the Callender family to piece together the story of a past tragedy which leads her into danger. The book takes place in 1894 and is written for the older and more able reader.

Biographical Fiction

*Felton, Harry. 1976. *Deborah Sampson: Soldier of the Revolution.* New York: Dodd.

Written for the middle grades, the author tells the story of the woman who donned men's clothing to serve in Washington's army.

Greenfield, Eloise. 1973. *Rosa Parks.* New York: Crowell.

Written for the younger child, this book tells the story of the determined woman who precipitated the Montgomery bus strike by refusing to follow the custom of blacks sitting in the rear of buses.

Monjo, F. N. 1987. *The One Bad Thing about Father.* New York: Trophy.

Written for the younger reader, this story gives a view of Theodore Roosevelt from his son's perspective.

Tobias, Tobi. 1975. *Arthur Mitchell.* New York: Crowell.

The founder of the Dance Theatre of Harlem overcame the bias against black ballet dancers through determination. The same author has also written a biography of the opera singer, Marian Anderson (1972).

Nonfiction: Exposition

Cole, Joanna. 1982. *A Bird's Body.* New York: William Morrow.

Joanna Cole has written a series of books for younger children, including *A Bird's Body* and *How a Dog Moves* (1985). Her writing is clear and adheres to scientific principles. The sharply focused photographs and diagrams help to explain the anatomical features.

Dabcovich, Lydia. 1985. *Sleepy Bear.* New York: E. P. Dutton.

In this simple story, autumn activities such as leaves falling and birds flying south are explained. The bear goes into a cave and sleeps through the winter and emerges in the spring.

Hoban, Tana. 1983. *Round & Round & Round.* New York: Greenwillow Books.

This book for young children demonstrates with color photographs the meaning of round by showing many common objects with that shape.

———. 1987. *I Read Signs.* New York: Mulberry.

This book has no text other than words shown in the pictures. It gives children an opportunity to read words they see regularly in their environment. The clear and colorful photographs of common signs such as "stop," "exit," and "don't walk" help the child understand the meaning of these functional words.

Simon, Seymour. 1985. *Jupiter.* New York: William Morrow.

This book gives the young reader a close-up look at this strange and mysterious planet. The text is clear and informative and includes twenty vivid photographs. Other astronomy books by the same author include *The Moon* (1984) and *Earth: Our Planet in Space* (1984).

Nonfiction: Argument†

Barry, Scott. 1979. *The Kingdom of Wolves.* New York: Putnam.

The author describes the life of the wolf and wolf pack, and through the use of photographs and text, pleads for the protection of wolves.

*Ford, Barbara. 1981. *Alligators, Raccoons, and Other Survivors: The Wildlife of the Future.* New York: William Morrow.

The author shows how humans have encroached on wildlife and argues that people must be more respectful of wildlife.

*Graham, Ada, and Frank Graham. 1981. *The Changing Desert.* New York: Scribner's.

This text-like book explains problems in the desert caused by vehicles, water, and overgrazing.

Miles, Betty. 1974. *Save the Earth! An Ecology Handbook for Kids.* New York: Knopf.

Activities are described that help children explore, appreciate, and protect their environment.

Scott, Jack. 1979. *The Book of the Goat.* New York: Putnam.

The author persuades the reader that the goat is a valuable and intelligent animal which is useful to humans.

---

† Very few children's books can be classified wholly as argument. These books present authors' points of view on particular issues.

References

Anderson, R. C., and W. B. Brown. 1975. On Asking People Questions about What They Are Reading. In *Psychology of Learning and Motivation,* edited by G. H. Bower. New York: Academic Press.

Baker, L., and Ann Brown. 1984. Cognitive Monitoring in Reading. In *Understanding Reading Comprehension Cognition, Language, and the Structure of Prose,* edited by J. Flood. Newark, Del.: International Reading Association.

Brown, Ann. 1985. Metacognition: The Development of Selective Attention Strategies for Learning from Texts. In *Theoretical Models and Processes of Reading,* 3d ed., edited by H. Singer and R. Raddell. Newark, Del.: International Reading Association.

Gaskins, Irene, and Jonathan Baron. 1985. Teaching Poor Readers to Cope with Maladaptive Cognitive Styles: A Training Program. *Journal of Learning Disabilities* 18:390–94.

Orasanu, J., editor. 1986. *Reading Comprehension: From Research to Practice.* Hillsdale, N.J.: Erlbaum.

Pearson, P. David, editor. 1984. *Handbook of Reading Research.* New York: Longman.

Santa, C. M., and B. L. Hayes, editors. 1981. *Children Prose Comprehension: Research and Practice.* Newark, Del.: International Reading Association.

Singer, H., and R. Raddell, editors. 1985. *Theoretical Models and Processes of Reading.* 3d ed. Newark, Del.: International Reading Association.

Related Readings

Barron, Pamela, and Jennifer Burley. 1984. *Jump Over the Moon.* New York: Holt, Rinehart and Winston.

This anthology is devoted solely to picture books. The book's arrangement is based on the developmental needs of children. "Mother Goose" volumes are the first picture books introduced, followed by poetry, alphabet and counting books, wordless picture books, informational books, realistic fiction, and folktales. Articles discuss the use of illustrations, storytelling, and how to share picture books.

Burke, Eileen. 1986. *Early Childhood Literature: For Love of Child and Book.* Needham Heights, Mass.: Allyn and Bacon.

The joy of sharing literature and the pleasure it brings to children pervade this book. The text focuses on three- to eight-year-old children and includes numerous anecdotes about young children's experiences with books.

Glazer, Joan I. 1986. *Literature for Young Children.* 2d ed. Columbus, Ohio: Charles E. Merrill.

This focuses on the opportunities books offer for supporting young children's language, intellectual, personality, social and moral, and aesthetic and creative development. A range of literature for children is introduced. The book is designed for teachers of preschool and primary-age children, and specific teaching strategies are offered.

Norton, Donna. 1987. *Through the Eyes of a Child: An Introduction to Children's Literature*. Columbus, Ohio: Charles E. Merrill.

This comprehensive text includes a history of children's literature, criteria for evaluating and selecting children's literature, and chapters on each of the genres, as well as chapters on multiethnic literature and artists and illustrations. Teaching suggestions, activities, and annotated bibliographies are included in each chapter.

Stewig, John Warren. 1988. *Children and Literature*. Boston: Houghton Mifflin.

Organized by genre, this text includes classroom strategies as an integral part of each chapter, augmented by extensive samples of children's oral and written responses to literature. There is a separate chapter devoted to wordless books, and another that focuses on helping boys and girls study visual elements in picture books.

Sutherland, Zena, and May Hill Arbuthnot. 1986. *Children and Books*. 7th ed. Glenview, Ill.: Scott, Foresman.

This comprehensive text includes sections about knowing children and books and exploring types of literature. There are suggestions on bringing children and books together, and major areas and issues in children's literature are addressed. Annotated booklists are organized by genre.

4 Book Illustration: Key to Visual and Oral Literacy

John Warren Stewig
University of Wisconsin–Milwaukee

The first three chapters dealt with the building blocks of literature: words and larger literary elements. But children's literature is not simply language. Usually the author's intent is augmented by illustrations, which extend and enhance concepts. We sometimes erroneously assume that children understand and appreciate the pictures that accompany literature. Unless we help children become aware of illustrations as an extension of the story, we may miss opportunities to increase literacy.

In the preceding chapter Helen Felsenthal suggested a strategy for approaching literature. In this chapter, John Warren Stewig presents an approach to the pictures that accompany the literature. Apart from some simple identification questions, teachers seldom ask children to seriously study pictures. We must develop ways to encourage children to interact with the illustrations so the artist can then provide additional content and comment, adding richly to the readers' understanding and enjoyment of the story.

Those who teach children to read are keenly aware of the word *literacy*, that elusive goal toward which we work. Much effort has been expended and many words written about achieving reading literacy—the ability to decode and utilize what is decoded. Most definitions of literacy include being able to read and write. Our colleagues in language arts have expended similar lavish amounts of time on ways to help children achieve written literacy.

Yet such efforts are incomplete, since they do not include an important component: visual and oral literacy. To be truly literate, especially in today's society, we must be able to decode messages in pictures and to encode our findings in oral language. How can such an assertion be justified?

Pervasiveness of Visuals

Debes and Williams (1974) point out that about eighty percent of our information comes to us visually. Our bombardment by visual stimuli is so universal it hardly evokes comment. Yet where in the curriculum do we teach children to "read" such visual input—to examine it carefully part by part, extracting meaning and interacting with what is extracted? Such processes are central to the reading program, but few children learn to read pictures effectively.

Developing Oral Literacy

A second important factor is developing oral literacy: the ability to put coherent thoughts into words, words into sentences, and sentences into larger units. We have known for some time that most of us spend more time communicating orally than in either reading or writing (Stewig 1983). Yet where in the elementary curriculum do we help children learn to express in words what they have taken in through their senses? Specifically, where do we help children learn to talk cogently and literately about what they see in pictures and other visual stimuli?

Approaches to visual and oral literacy instruction are as yet a mosaic of interesting ideas, rather than a coherent philosophy or a unified approach to educating young children. One pair of authors, in describing a visual literacy program, commented:

> Especially after the early grades, there is a tendency to minimize
> the visual aspects of communication and children are, in a sense,
> "weaned away" from pictures and illustrations . . . (Fransecky
> and Debes 1972, 23)

If children are seldom encouraged to study illustrations, they are even less often asked to translate what they have learned in this visual mode into the oral mode. Putting thoughts about what was learned visually into spoken words is an important challenge all children should experience. Byars (1984) points out how important verbalizing about what is seen can be in the development of thinking skills.

Visual/Oral Skills

In developing visual/oral literacy, there are three subskills to be considered. These are sequential, from simple to more complex, and children should have opportunities to develop one skill before moving to the next one.

Describe What You See

The first of these skills is for the child to describe objectively—clearly, concisely, concretely—what he or she sees. It is apparent that another *C*, a commonly advanced purpose for elementary education—creativity—is not included here. As there are times, according to Evans (1967) when creativity in children's writing is unimportant if not irrelevant, so there are times in oral language when the crucial task is observing accurately and then describing with clarity. What we are asking children to do is to study an object providing visual input, then translate this input into words.

Compare Two Different Objects

The second skill is an extension of the first—to compare two different objects using common descriptors. That is, given two objects, can the child accurately describe the two, including the differences that exist? A logical way to begin this process with young children is to provide opportunities for them to observe their classmates and then describe what they have noticed. Or, in looking at two pictures, can the child see what is similar about them, and what sets them apart from each other? If we have two versions of *Little Red Riding Hood,* can children describe how Little Red is the same or different in the pictures? Experts in thinking skills identify comparing/contrasting as a central skill (Byars 1983).

Value One of the Pictures

The third, more sophisticated, and most important of these visual/oral skills is the ability to value one of the objects. We want children to develop the ability to say which picture they prefer, and why. This ability is important because few are capable of more than an impoverished description of their evaluations. Listen to adults tell you what they like. Inchoate thoughts too often come out as insistent reiterations of what a person "likes." Indeed, it is a rare individual who can give a convincing reason for a visual preference. The adult who insists, "I don't really know anything about art, but I know what I like," is not only telling the listener about an impoverished background, but also about a muddled thought process and a paucity of verbal expression.

Believing, then, that this three-part ability is crucial for adults and possible for children, what kinds of experiences should classroom teachers plan to develop children's visual/oral literacy?

Materials to Use

Some writers describing the possibilities in visual literacy recommend film study. This is indeed exciting after preparatory experiences. For young children, however, such visual images on film move too quickly and are not conducive to study and reflection. Additional drawbacks are the cost and relative inconvenience of film.

As an alternative, a plentiful, convenient, and relatively inexpensive source of material exists: illustrations in children's books. Much of what we do with developing visual and oral skills can be done through this medium. Countless artists work in the field, and picture and illustrated books proliferate. The teacher is at no loss, therefore, to find materials children may use in developing these skills.

It is a simple task to locate several different artists' illustrations of the same story or poem as a basis for practicing each of the three skills. *Cinderella, Rumpelstiltskin, Chanticleer and the Fox*—these and countless other tales have inspired artists to create their own versions of the story. Poetry has also received attention from artists. Such well-known poems as Lear's "The Owl and the Pussycat" have been illustrated by several artists and can serve as the basis for describing, comparing, and valuing experiences.

Variety in Style

Using pictures from books as stimulus material, the teacher is helping children study the illustrations as a separate entity, not merely for the extension or augmentation they provide for the text. Each should be examined as an independent visual artifact with meaning of its own. With young children begin very simply, using one illustration and asking them to tell what they see, to detail what they take in visually.

The Three Billy Goats Gruff is a logical starting point in working with kindergarten or first-grade children. Locate a variety of illustrations for the story, and then ask children to tell what they see. The teacher may focus attention on the visual treatment of the goats. The bold rendering in casein by Stobbs (1967) is quite unlike the dainty hoofed goat by Lenski (Hutchinson 1925). The rakish mien of one goat (Asbjornsen and Moe 1957), sketched casually by Marcia Brown in fluid ink line, is different from the precise black designs by Vroman (Asbjornsen and Moe 1963). Different from any of these are the brown and white goats by the d'Aulaires (1969), crossing in trio above a huge troll.

At another time attention might be focused on the troll, an unloved and too frequently ignored soul. One artist portrayed him as a gargantuan creature, another as a long-nosed and hairy being, still another as brooding and almost perplexed. One artist shows a fey creature scarcely likely to devour the goats.

Another favorite of the young child is *Little Red Riding Hood.* The visual treatment of Little Red varies from the stolid interpretation by Bruna (1966), through the pixie created in lithography by Jean Merrill (1968), to the apprehensive little girl overwhelmed by the encompassing forest drawn by Aloise (Gant and Gant 1969). Peris (1986) uses pleasantly simple watercolors with only enough detail to define, not overwhelm. The scene in the bedchamber with both the wolf and Little Red brings forth many responses. Children often comment on the many-patterned quilt and plaid bedhangings provided by Trina Schart Hyman (1983). One child commented that she liked the Pincus (1968) version because "Little Red Riding Hood and the wolf are both so funny looking." Another said, "I like this one better because there's so much to look at in it." In looking at the picture by Hogrogian (1967), one child commented, "Little Red should have the glasses on. Then she could see by the big nose that it's a wolf and not grandma."

After children have had several experiences describing what they see in pictures, they can move to the next skill, which is comparing two pictures for the same story or poem. In all these experiences, children are learning to absorb impressions through their sense of sight, then give oral expression to their observations and comparisons.

A favorite of older children, *Cinderella,* works well for comparison purposes. Hogrogian's (1981) version presents all the pictures inside patterned frames, while Alan Suddon's (1969) version features whimsical collage pictures which extend to the page edges. Brown's (1954) watercolor wash treatment depicts both the consideration of the prince and the dismay of the sisters. We sometimes encourage children to compare the illustrative treatment of the prince. The prince by Ness (Haviland 1965), in bold modern robes and unfortunately large feet, is very different from the one by Brown (1954). The luxuriant patterning evident in Ness's woodcuts captures and holds children's attention as they explore the wealth of visual detail. Encourage the children to compare and contrast the ball gowns of Cinderella. One girl said of the romantic yet gothic illustration by Arthur Rackham (1950), "Her dress is so fluffy it looks like it could float to the ball by itself." When studying the illustration in Lang's book (1948), another girl wondered how Cinderella could run fast in such a skirt.

Puss in Boots is an old tale that never fails to amuse children, who delight in the sly cat's efforts to trick people. Some versions are done in simple black and white (Huber 1965); yet even when the color is limited and the technique is similar, there are discernible differences in interpretation (Johnson 1961). The lithographs of Brown's (1952) debonair cat and Fischer's (1959) striped one, both limited in color, nevertheless are favorites of children and do stimulate oral description. More complex treatments good for comparison purposes also show wide variety of style (Haviland 1959). One child remarked of this version, "I like this one because it looks like it happened in a foreign country" (Kastner 1957). Any of these versions with words might be compared with a variant by Rodriguez (1985), an interesting attempt in the "Tell Me a Story" series which presents the tales in a small (about 6" × 7") format, without words. Rodriguez's *Puss in Boots* in this set of six tales is more effective than the *Cinderella,* as it is less consciously sweet.

The familiar story of *Goldilocks and the Three Bears* has challenged the talents of many artists, ranging from favorite old illustrations by Arthur Rackham to more recent versions by Anne Rockwell (1975) and by Janet Stevens (1986). Sometimes the bears remain animals, as in the illustrations by Rackham (1950). At other times they are made very human; Lenski (Hutchinson 1925) clothes her family, as does Stobbs (1965).

Comparing the treatment of the central character facilitates developing oral language fluency. Three artists show Goldilocks sampling the porridge, yet in each case the illustration is very unlike the others (Cauley 1981; Rojankovsky 1948; Carruth 1962). This old tale also is useful in demonstrating for children the idea of story variation. Folk and fairy tales are available in many versions. This story, unlike others, can be traced to a specific author, Eleanor Mure (1967, photographic reproduction of handlettered original) who originally wrote and illustrated her story in 1831. In her version, the intruder was not a sweet child, but rather a greedy old woman. The incensed bears, not content with chasing her from the house, tried to do away with her in the fireplace. To their dismay, they discovered she was noncombustible. The Andrew Lang (1949) version also depicts an irascible old lady, not dismayed, but in fact rather annoyed at having

Copyright: Hans Fischer, *Der gestiefelte Kater.* Artemis Verlag, Zürich, 1966.

her sleep interrupted. Still another mutation of the story, which captivates children but arouses the wrath of some of their teachers, is the one by Tony Palazzo (1959). He depicts a conventional enough trio of bears, but a highly unconventional Goldilocks, a long-haired dog! More recently Bernadette Watts (1985) illustrated fairly conventionally, but nonetheless pleasantly, an oversized version with double-page spreads.

Teachers might choose any of the editions described here, though there are others which could also be used. To locate a variety of editions, see the book by MacDonald (1982), which lists more than three hundred individual picture books.

Using Poetry

The illustrations for many poems are also helpful in motivating children in the process of describing, comparing, and valuing. For

Reprinted by permission of Charles Scribner's Sons, an imprint of Macmillan Publishing Company from PUSS IN BOOTS written and illustrated by Marcia Brown. Copyright 1952 Marcia Brown; copyright renewed 1980.

example, several illustrations are available for many poems. Two that can serve as examples of this are "The Owl and the Pussycat" and "Old Mother Hubbard."

The nonsense of Lear's poem, "The Owl and the Pussycat" (1961), has intrigued many artists, beginning with the poet himself. Lear's illustrations are of interest historically, but do not capture children's attention and motivate oral language as easily as do other versions. For example, contrast them with the contemporary open color illustrations of Cooney (1961) which evoke a lush forest repast. Her pictures for this poem are also available in a French version, which can be used with children to reinforce the idea that people write and read different languages, an important aid in guiding children away from the ethnocentrism so natural to them when they are young. Arnold Lobel (1983) did four small pictures showing the sequence of action down one side of a page in a poetry collection. Larger pictures by Gwen Fulton (1977) are full of details that create an almost surrealistic effect. Hilary Knight (1983) sets the poem in a frame-story about Professor Comfort and his young guests Polly and Otto, to whom the professor reads the poem. In this version the walls dissolve, a la *Where the Wild Things Are,* and the children are drawn into the adventure, becoming the animal characters.

Other versions of this frequently illustrated poem include one by Janet Stevens (1983), in pastel shades overlaid with pencil to give detail and dimension in double-page spreads bled to the edge. Lorinda Cauley's (1986) version features less completely clothed animals, which also less completely dominate their pages, resulting in a more relaxed set of drawings than those by Stevens. Owen Wood's (1986) pictures pile quasi-Victorian detail upon detail until viewers have to search for the characters and the central action: this edition is not for the claustrophobic! Finally, a miniature (4″ × 5″) format with full color, mostly pastel illustrations bordered with a thin black rule, features simplified, somewhat abstract animals in an edition by Emma Crosby (1986).

Mother Goose rhymes also offer rich possibilities for developing oral facility. "Old Mother Hubbard" has been illustrated by a variety of artists. Though in most drawings she is in cap and apron, there the similarities stop, and wide differences in interpretation are available. Some are in black and white, as is the one by Rackham (1969), while some are in full color, as is the one by Tenggren (1940). Some feature an old woman of ample proportions; Galdone's (1960) hefty mother sports a fashionable bustle and gingham apron. Ward's illustration (Huber 1965) depicts her as tall, while Lobel's (1968) version shows a compact dumpling of a woman. James Marshall's (1986) mother is equally rotund in flat pastel colors enclosed in a firm black line. Even the evocation of time is different. In comparing two illustrations, one child felt that the one by deAngeli (1955) "... looks like it happened longer ago," contrasted with the one by Rojankovsky (1942).

Children's Response to the Materials

Once the teacher has selected a variety of illustrations to use with children and is ready to begin, how should the materials be used? How can the children be expected to respond?

Specific methods of presentation, types of questions used to stimulate observation and discussion, number of illustrations used, and length of the sessions must depend on the group. The teacher will vary these factors in sessions that develop skills of describing, leading to oral literacy.

While using "The Owl and the Pussycat," I discovered that kindergarten children without previous experience in structured oral discussion delighted in describing what they saw in illustrations for the nonsense verse by Lear. They were developing the first skill needed for visual/oral literacy—that of describing. Since it was an initial experience, we began simply with one illustration and a few questions:

1. What do you see in the picture?
2. What colors has the artist used?
3. Where is this event taking place? How can you tell?
4. What things did the owl and pussycat take along?
5. Is the boat like any you have seen? How different is it?

Sixth graders, who had a variety of previous oral language experiences, did quite well in evaluating as a result of close observation and practice in describing. A classroom teacher used two illustrations for *Peter and the Wolf* in doing a three-section unit on describing. The pictures were put up in the room for a few days so children could observe them. Children responded well to the challenge of seeing how closely they could discern what was in the pictures. One oral discussion session centered on describing, separately, each illustration. A second session centered on comparing the illustrations. Children were encouraged to make notes so they could speak informally from their papers. During the third session, children explained their reasons for preferring, or *valuing*, one of the illustrations. In a tape-recorded response to the illustrations, Mark chose the book by Mikolaycak (1982):

> I personally like Mikolaycak better than Voigt because his story looked and seemed more realistic.

> The pictures were far better with Mikolaycak than Voigt. Mikolaycak's pictures were more lifelike and had more interesting detail to it, like Peter's house with the little red gate in the front. On the other hand, Voigt's book was sort of plain. Peter's house looked like a simple cottage.

> Another comparison is on the characters. Expressions on the faces of the characters are more like in real life in Mikolaycak's book. The grandfather has wrinkles and when he's mad he looks mad. But in Voigt's story the grandfather looks like a young person with a fake beard on.

In contrast, Jenny chose the Voigt (1980) illustration.

> I support Voigt because the illustrations have a lot of detail. People were smaller and there is a lot of color added. To me

From *Peter and the Wolf*, adapted from the musical tale by Sergei Prokofiev, illustrations by Erna Voight. Copyright © 1979 by Annette Betz Verlag. Reprinted by permission of David R. Godine, Publishers.

the pictures look like oil paintings which I really like to look at.
Voigt has nice pictures and to top that I like the little instruments
at the bottom; it's really groovy. It's also interesting to read. If
I could grade the illustrations I'd give it an *A+*. There is nothing
I don't like about the illustrations. I think the scenery is just
perfect. There is no other book I like as much. It has a lot of
background. Nice blue clouds, wonderful pictures, the best. I
like the book so much. I want it for my own just to page through
and just look at the pictures. The scenes are plain wonderful.
It has a beautiful young boy and young hunters. The little cat
is beautiful; the wolf is very sly. I really love the pictures.

There was little verbal impoverishment apparent as these sixth graders
discussed articulately the reasons for their choices.

In each of these briefly described examples, the third, or valuing
stage, was simply involving children in a subjective, personal response
to what they had seen and reflected upon. That was appropriate
because the teachers had just begun working with the students on
visual/oral literacy. It is possible, however, over a period of time, to
work with children in a methodical study of such visual elements as
line, shape, color, form, and dimension, to develop a more sophisticated critical ability in children (Stewig 1988–89). The Getty Center
(1985) reports impressive new work in this area by art teachers,
though the methodology has not yet been widely used and reported
upon by classroom teachers.

Developing Typeface Awareness

Another technique for developing visual sensitivity which challenges
children to put into words what they have perceived is planned
experiences with typefaces. There is rich variety, with both subtle
and readily apparent differences, available today. The novelty of
studying something they have seldom thought about intrigues children. In the process, they sharpen visual perception skills and verbal
abilities.

Two readily available sources for typeface samples exist:

1. Most magazines contain a wide variety of type samples, especially
    in advertisements. Close inspection of typeface samples taken
    from magazine advertisements will reveal differences that aren't
    apparent at first glance (Figure 1).

2. Children's books also contain such variety; these can be enlarged
    by an opaque projector to make them big enough to use.

The paper is outstanding.

We are proud of you.

Figure 1. Typeface examples reveal differences that are not apparent at first glance.

Such a unit of study might begin with a trip to a local printer. A logical follow-up might be some brief investigation of the history and development of movable type, appropriate to the grade level involved. Then the teacher can introduce activities to increase visual sensitivity, presenting a variety of typefaces of quite different styles. (A single

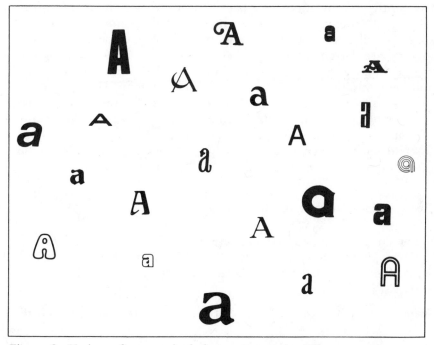

Figure 2. Variety of ways a single letter appears in different typefaces.

letter can be printed in a variety of ways, as shown in Figure 2.) The problem for the children is to notice the physical characteristics of the typeface, and to describe in words the differences they have perceived. As children's ability to describe their perceptions develops, the differences in the samples grow smaller. Interspersed with such teacher-initiated sessions, or perhaps following them, are experiences in which children search for samples of typefaces and then group them according to criteria like thick/thin, tall/short, light/heavy, and serif/sans serif, among others. Visual sophistication in detecting similarities and differences and the ability to categorize grow as children experience a series of such activities. Along with this growth is the increasing power of translating into words the visual sensations children have experienced.

Summary

Visual and oral literacy skills, so crucial because they are the most frequently used by adults, are paradoxically among those least often developed systematically in elementary schools. Among several reasons for this is the fact that component subskills of visual and oral literacy are infrequently identified. Because all three subskills are crucial, children must be provided opportunities to *describe, compare,* and *value* orally. One effective way of encouraging children to do this is to use illustrations from children's literature; another approach is to involve them in typeface study. Both approaches offer many advantages: materials are easy to locate, plentiful, and of much interest to children. Children respond eagerly to these methods and in the process develop valuable visual and oral literacy skills.

Recommended Books for Classroom Use

These children's books, cited as references in this chapter, are useful in developing visual and oral literacy skills. Teachers should note that some titles are keyed by the illustrator's name, rather than by the author's.

Asbjornsen, P. C., and J. E. Moe. 1957. *The Three Billy Goats Gruff.* New York: Harcourt.

———. 1983. *East of the Sun and West of the Moon.* New York: Macmillan.
Blair, Susan. 1963. *Three Billy Goats Gruff.* New York: Holt.

Brown, Marcia. 1952. *Puss in Boots.* New York: Scribner's.

———. 1954. *Cinderella.* New York: Scribner's.

Bruna, Dick. 1966. *Little Red Riding Hood.* Chicago: Follett.

Carruth, J., editor. 1962. *My Book of Goldilocks and the Three Bears.* New York: Maxton.

Cauley, Lorinda Bryan. 1981. *Goldilocks and the Three Bears.* New York: Putnam's.

———. 1986. *The Owl and the Pussycat.* New York: Putnam.

Cooney, Barbara. 1961. *The Owl and the Pussy Cat.* Boston: Little, Brown.

Crosby, Emma. 1986. *The Owl and the Pussycat.* Manchester, N.H.: Salem House.

d'Aulaire, Ingri, and Edgar Parin. 1969. *Twenty-One Norwegian Folk Tales.* New York: Viking.

deAngeli, Marguerite. 1955. *Book of Nursery and Mother Goose Rhymes.* New York: Doubleday.

Fischer, Hans. 1959. *Puss in Boots.* New York: Harcourt.

Fulton, Gwen, illustrator. 1977. *The Owl and the Pussy-Cat.* New York: Atheneum.

Galdone, Paul. 1960. *Old Mother Hubbard and Her Dog.* New York: Whittlesey House.

Gant, Elizabeth, and Katherine Gant. 1969. *Little Red Riding Hood.* Nashville: Abingdon.

Haviland, Virginia. 1959. *Favorite Fairy Tales Told in France.* Toronto: Little, Brown.

———. 1965. *Favorite Fairy Tales Told in Italy.* Boston: Little.

Hogrogian, Nonny. 1967. *The Renowned History of Little Red Riding Hood.* New York: Crowell.

———. 1981. *Cinderella.* New York: Greenwillow Books.

Huber, M. B. 1965. *Story and Verse for Children.* New York: Macmillan.

Hutchinson, editor. 1925. *Chimney Corner Stories.* New York: Minton, Balch.

Hyman, Trina Schart. 1982. *Little Red Riding Hood.* New York: Holiday House.

Johnson, A. E., translator. 1961. *Perrault's Complete Fairy Tales.* New York: Mead.

Kastner, Erich. 1957. *Puss in Boots.* New York: Julian Messner.

Knight, Hilary. 1983. *The Owl and the Pussy-cat.* New York: Macmillan.

Lang, Andrew. 1948. *The Blue Fairy Book*. New York: David McKay.

————. 1949. *The Green Fairy Book*. London: Longmans, Green.

Lear, Edward. 1961. *The Owl and the Pussy Cat*. New York: Little, Brown.

Lobel, Arnold. 1968. *The Comic Adventures of Old Mother Hubbard and Her Dog*. New York: Bradbury.

Lobel, Arnold, illustrator. 1983. *The Random House Book of Poetry*. New York: Random House.

Marshall, James. 1986. *Mother Goose*. New York: Sunburst.

Merrill, Jean, and Ronni Solbert. 1968. *Red Riding Hood*. New York: Pantheon.

Mikolaycak, Charles. 1982. *Peter and the Wolf*. New York: Viking.

Mure, Eleanor. 1967. *The Story of the Three Bears*. New York: H. Z. Walck.

Palazzo, Tony. 1959. *Goldilocks and the Three Bears*. Garden City, N.Y.: Doubleday.

Peris, Carme. 1986. *Little Red Riding Hood*. Morristown, N.J.: Silver Burdett.

Pincus, Harriet. 1968. *Little Red Riding Hood*. New York: Harcourt.

Rackham, Arthur. 1950. *The Arthur Rackham Fairy Book*. New York: Lippincott.

Rackham, Arthur, illustrator. 1969. *Mother Goose Rhymes*. New York: Franklin Watts.

Rockwell, Anne, illustrator. 1975. *The Three Bears and Fifteen Other Stories*. New York: Crowell.

Rodriguez, Conxita. 1985. *Puss in Boots*. Morristown, N.J.: Silver Burdett.

Rojankovsky, F. 1942. *The Tall Book of Mother Goose*. New York: Harper.

————. 1948. *The Three Bears*. New York: Simon and Schuster.

Stevens, Janet. 1983. *The Owl and the Pussycat*. New York: Holiday House.

————. 1986. *Goldilocks and the Three Bears*. New York: Holiday House.

Stobbs, William. 1965. *The Three Bears*. New York: Whittlesley House.

————. 1967. *Three Billy Goats Gruff*. New York: McGraw-Hill.

Suddon, Alan. 1969. *Cinderella*. London: Dennis Dobson.

Tenggren. 1940. *Mother Goose*. Toronto: Little, Brown.

The Three Bears. 1955. Racine, Wis.: Whitman.

Voigt, Erna. 1980. *Peter and the Wolf*. Boston: David R. Godine.

Watts, Bernadette. 1985. *Goldilocks and the Three Bears.* New York: North-South Books.

Wood, Owen. 1986. *The Owl and the Pussy-Cat and Other Nonsense.* Morristown, N.J.: Silver Burdett.

References

Byars, Barry K. 1983. Common Sense about Teaching Thinking Skills. *Educational Leadership* 41:44–49.

————. 1984. Improving Thinking Skills—Practical Approaches. *Phi Delta Kappan* 66:556–60.

Debes, John L., and Clarence M. Williams. 1974. The Power of Visuals. *Instructor* 84:32–38.

Evans, Robert. 1967. A Glove Thrown Down. *Elementary English,* May, 523–27.

Fransecky, Roger B., and John L. Debes. 1972. *Visual Literacy: A Way to Learn—A Way to Teach.* Washington, D.C.: Association for Education Communication and Technology.

Getty Center for Education in the Arts. 1985. *Beyond Creating: The Place for Art in America's Schools.* Los Angeles: The Getty Center.

MacDonald, Margaret Read. 1982. *Storyteller's Source Book: A Subject, Title, and Motif Index to Folklore Collections for Children.* Detroit: Gale Research.

Stewig, John Warren. 1983. *Exploring Language Arts in the Elementary Classroom.* New York: Richard C. Owen.

————. 1988–89. *Reading Pictures: Exploring Illustrations with Children* series. Milwaukee, Wis.: Jenson Publications.

Related Readings

Alderson, Brian. 1973. *Looking at Picture-Books, 1973; An Exhibition Prepared by Brian Alderson and Arranged by the National Book League.* Distributed in the United States by Children's Book Council.

Annotations in this exhibition catalogue are refreshing because they are critical, rather than simply descriptive. The author evaluates the books, not just telling what each includes. Though primarily British in focus, the large number of books also published in the United States makes this a valuable resource. Books are arranged in categories, and a brief (two or three paragraphs) introduction precedes each category. Though the black and white illustrations are small, the juxtaposition of several contrasting ones on the same page clarifies the text.

Bader, Barbara. 1976. *American Picturebooks from Noah's Ark to The Beast Within.* New York: Macmillan.

A generous size, clear illustrations in quantity, and an articulate text mark this as the definitive book on the subject. Bader writes convincingly, sharing the results of years of study and a perceptive view. The book helps one see today's picture books in light of historical antecedents, all too often inaccessible to anyone but scholars. Unlike many books of criticism, this is neither dry nor pedantic: for even the novice it makes engrossing reading.

Crago, Maureen, and Hugh Crago. 1983. Order from Chaos: Learning to Read Pictures. In *Prelude to Literacy*, 143–62. Carbondale: Southern Illinois University Press.

Learning to read pictures is as complex as learning to read print. The authors document the literacy learning of their daughter over the extended time period they kept journals about the process. The authors detail the kind of "preconceptions" that support or interfere with children's reading pictures. Visual miscues often result from misinterpretation of figure/ ground relationships, and the authors give several of these, tied to specific books. Shape distortions due to viewing angle are discussed, as are size differences of objects seen from close up and far away. Changes in object size on succeeding pages are another visual convention children must learn. Consistency and accuracy of color sometimes also interfere with visual understanding. Objects chopped off by the page edge demonstrate another artistic convention that perplexes child viewers. The authors conclude this in-depth analysis of their child's visual development by stating that "by the time she was 5.0, she had served an apprenticeship and seldom wanted any explanations of what was happening in an illustration."

Egoff, Sheila A. 1981. Picture Books. In *Thursday's Child*, 247–74. Chicago: American Library Association.

Contending that picture books are subjected to closer scrutiny and more judgment than any other genre, Egoff asserts a paradox: though they seem to be the "Coziest and most gentle of genres . . ." they actually produce the greatest social and aesthetic tensions in all of children's literature. Setting this argument in the context of changes that occurred during the fertile period from 1930 through 1960, she notes a balance between words and pictures that now seems to have given way to excessive emphasis on the pictorial. In addition to comments about visual aspects of the form, she notes the psychological change that has taken place. Citing Sendak's *Where the Wild Things Are*, she notes the move from the secure, childlike experiences brought to resolution (present in earlier books), to the cathartic view in which picture books are a vehicle for the portrayal of "specific and complex aspects of childhood darkness." Egoff feels the economic recession of the 1970s had a positive effect on picture books: artists must be more ingenious within narrower limits, resulting in books of childlike simplicity. She questions whether this format can really support the serious themes being attempted: the power of the book as a teaching vehicle has come into its own again, as publishers and authors load up these small-scale books with messages. In closing, she notes the widening audience for picture books; while this form seems to be leading the way in innovation, some artists (like Burningham, Marshall, and Waber) continue to produce satisfying works in the established tradition.

Larkin, David. 1974. *The Fantastic Kingdom*. New York: Ballantine.

In beautifully clear, intriguingly colored full-page reproductions, the editor presents fourteen illustrators whose names are too often unknown, their paintings forgotten. All born in the last half of the nineteenth century, they created a unique world of fantasy, infused with elements of Art Nouveau. Despite that common element, there is remarkable diversity here, which will delight the student of children's book illustration.

Meyer, Susan E. 1983. *A Treasury of the Great Children's Book Illustrators.* New York: Abrams.

An extended introduction considers the time setting and the social and economic conditions that influenced the flowering of children's book illustration. The author later augments this with studies of thirteen particular illustrators. An admittedly idiosyncratic book, this leaves living, contemporary illustrators to the body of children's literature specialists from whom Meyer is careful to distance herself. Social changes, particularly manufacturing, which during Victorian times changed the face of England forever, are Meyer's first topic. This leads to consideration of the child in the context of the Victorian family, and of antecedents to modern publishing, both considered briefly. For most readers the material on the adult aesthetic ferment of the times (i.e., such pre-Raphaelites as John Ruskin) will be unfamiliar.

In a section on illustrators, Meyer gives a brief look ahead to the fuller chapters later. Despite the fact that these artists were all Victorians, there were notable differences. N. C. Wyeth "preferred to illustrate the scene as it was described in words"; Arthur Rackham "preferred to illustrate the indescribable"; Randolph Caldecott "chose to weave his pictures in and out of the words"; and both Walter Crane and W. W. Denslow thought "the words themselves were part of the total picture [integrating] exquisitely designed letterforms."

Individual chapters about illustrators, ranging from fourteen pages on Caldecott to twenty-two pages for Howard Pyle, are lavishly illustrated with full-color reproductions. In fact, the Caldecott chapter has almost more pictures than text. There are detailed considerations of the illustrator's career, influences, and important commissions; less attention is devoted to critical comments on why the person is "great."

Nodelman, Perry. 1988. *Words about Pictures. The Narrative Art of Children's Picture Books.* Athens, Ga.: The University of Georgia Press.

Clearly the most definitive and exhaustive examination of how children receive, process, and react to illustrations, this—though not a book concerned with methodology—nonetheless has many implications for how teachers work with children. Nodelman examines pictures (what is included, what is left out, what it is assumed child viewers know); their style (as related to art movements, and as style is shaped by such visual elements as line, shape, color, etc.); and how what we know about child development should affect what we do in helping children become more literate viewers. Because the book includes only a few black-and-white illustrations, it needs to be read with the actual children's books described at hand, in order to more clearly understand Nodelman's many valuable insights.

Shulevitz, Uri. 1985. *Writing with Pictures: How to Write and Illustrate Children's Books.* New York: Watson-Guptill.

Shulevitz says visual thinking is the key to "writing with pictures," creating a flow of graphic images crucial in picture books. Illustrations must be readable, coherent, and obviously related to the text. The illustrator's obligation is to understand as fully as possible the needs of the book. This book is divided into four parts. To begin, Shulevitz distinguishes between the true picture book and the storybook with pictures. Part Two deals with technical concerns like storyboards and dummies, and the author then moves to more general concerns of the book's physical structure, including size, scale, and shape. In Part Three Shulevitz analyzes both purposes of illustrations and the art of drawing. Part Four becomes more technical, focusing on how books are made. The book demonstrates that Shulevitz is not only a consummate image maker: he is also a superb wordsmith. Over 600 illustrations accompany a volume that is logical, with language that communicates clearly.

5 Reading Leads to Writing

Richard G. Kolczynski
Ball State University

In this chapter, Richard G. Kolczynski deals with the way writing grows from reading. It is commonly asserted in professional literature that these two are interrelated, though the nature of that relation isn't often clarified. Kolczynski opens with a brief summary of the plethora of recent research on the composing process. He then identifies quite specifically the types of learning that occur as students read, are read to, and reflect on the reading. Increased sensitivity to language is one of the main outcomes of such experiences.

As children talk about writing possibilities after reading, models of literary forms are made clear, and students can begin to see the options they may choose when they write. The author follows this with a section on four techniques for helping children write in a variety of forms. The chapter concludes with a practical section on workshop settings in classrooms; in brief but encompassing scope Kolczynski is able to make this often recommended but seldom implemented suggestion possible for teachers.

There is no doubt that helping children read and write has gained public attention throughout our country and has become the central focus of education across all grades and subject areas. To list the values of increasing literacy would repeat the obvious, but what needs to be done and how can we do it?

Several studies, including those of the National Assessment of Educational Progress (1975, 1981) and by Graves (1978) for the Ford Foundation, have reported that students do not have significant problems with the conventions and mechanics of writing as much as with connected discourse. In too many classrooms, however, grammar, punctuation, penmanship, and workbook exercises have taken over, leaving little time for continuous and connected writing. The increased time spent on isolated skills practiced outside of concrete, functional, and ongoing activities has resulted in a deficiency in youngsters' abilities to express themselves in written form. The problem with writing, as Graves reports, is that there is no writing.

Reading instruction, similarly, is often limited to a skill and drill activity, focusing on bits of language extracted from discourse without meaningful context. Basal readers and workbooks are given priority, while the wide world of children's literature may be left to library visits and free reading sessions. After observing from a distance one second grader enjoying a book from cover to cover, displaying many reading-like behaviors that seemed to indicate an engrossed and active reader, I approached him and asked if he would share his book with me. Excited and eager, he began reading the cover information, proceeding with the text, pausing to see if I was following and ostensibly understanding, and pointing to pictures and words of special interest. I was impressed. I thought he had taken a course in storytelling and book sharing. "Surely you're in the highest reading group?" I asked. After a bit of confusion and a long pause, he informed me: "No. I'm good at library reading, but I'm in the bottom group in class 'cause of vols and constants [sic]." How many children claim the same?

Another student shared with me her enthusiasm for reading storybooks and poetry which provided her with ideas for her own creations. Unfortunately, she confessed, most of her reading and writing is limited to what she does at home. Why? "Everything we read in school we have to write a book report on, and I don't want to write about books; I want to write books." The writing experiences of too many children are limited to trite, single-topic assignments: book reports, copied and culled reports, and various other stifling exercises, void of personal meaning.

Today many educators agree that reading good literature and the experiences that flow from such reading can no longer be subsumed under "library" or "free reading" programs, or be left to what can be done at home. More attention, now more than ever before, should be given to reading and writing as an integral part of language arts which, in turn, can be integrated with the entire school program. Reading and writing need to be viewed as supportive and interactive processes whereby what is learned from reading can be used when writing, and what is learned by writing can foster an appreciation for authorship and reading. A good program, therefore, is a well-planned, continuing experience where children are read to by others and are encouraged to read for themselves. Such a program not only guides them in developing interests, knowledge, skills, and appreciation needed to enjoy literature, but opens up new vistas for their own self-expression.

Fortunately, educational theory and research over the past decade has shed new light on the talking, reading, and writing connection. Dyson's study (1981) helps us understand how oral language is an integral part of learning to write, providing meaning and the means for putting ideas on paper. Nancie Atwell (1984) provides evidence that children can learn more about reading and writing when they become "insiders"—active participants in those processes, establishing workshops where "kids and teachers write, read, and talk writing and reading" (240). Margaret Atwell (1980) points out the importance of the interaction between reading and writing as processes and the experience that evolves as a result of simultaneous interaction. DeFord's (1981) study of three first-grade classrooms offers significant insight into the effects of various language environments upon reading and writing. The "whole language" classroom, where teacher and children shared a variety of stories, poems, and books rather than basal texts, produced children who demonstrated deeper understanding and use of language as they became authors, learning the author's tasks and using literature as a model for other language experiences. Blount (1973) provides a review of earlier studies that show a positive relationship between good writing and increased reading experiences, while detailed descriptions of the important role of stories in beginning writing development can be found in studies conducted by King and Rentel (1982, 1983). And finally, excellent descriptions of the development of writing behavior can be found in Clay (1975), Graves (1983), and Calkins (1986).

These studies suggest several implications for classroom practice:

> Children need to be active participants in all phases of the writing process: prewriting, drafting, revising, editing, and sharing. The classroom environment should allow children to discover the interactive and recursive nature of writing.

> Children need to be surrounded by a variety of poems and books, both fiction and informational. Teachers and students need to become partners in sharing this literature. Students read aloud with partners or in groups as well as silently and independently. Talking and writing need to become natural forms of responding to reading.

> The classroom should be transformed into a writing workshop where children can observe each other as well as the teacher. All participants will take delight in sharing their writing when

completed, but most of what is learned about authorship will come from opportunities to share at each and every step along the way. Interacting with writers-at-work works! Teacher and peer conferences held before, during, and after writing offer much support and encouragement to aspiring authors.

The suggestions given throughout this chapter are based on the above premises. Although brief and concise, the ideas presented here will offer the imaginative and ambitious teacher a springboard for making a reading/writing connection. Additional sources of ideas and suggestions are included in the annotated "Related Readings" at the end of the chapter.

What Children Learn from Literature

One of the greatest values of a literature program is that it serves as a source for a variety of creative endeavors. In addition to being inspired to paint, dance, sing, or dramatize, children can be motivated to explore and expand their own capacity for personal writing. Just as children learn to speak and use their language by listening to those around them, they can also discover the values and applications of literature as an impetus for their own creative expression. Children cannot effectively tell or write about stories or books or create their own fiction, however, until they are exposed to good models of literature. The teacher, therefore, has the responsibility to provide time for a variety of literary experiences and to promote interest in and favorable attitudes toward fine literature. By listening to and reading good stories, poems, and books, children will develop a store of knowledge and experiences that will guide them as they discover the means to express their own ideas.

The most significant value of wide and continuous contact with literature is the development and refinement of children's sensitivity to language. Exposure to language, both oral and written, influences vocabulary development. Mollie Hunter (1976) recognizes that "words are inherently magical" and calls for children's authors to use colorful and vivid words in rhythmic patterns. Reading allows children to become aware of the function of words, figurative expressions, and sentence patterns. As children are guided in their explorations of literature, they will become increasingly aware of the functional and creative attributes of language, and they should be helped in their attempts to use language expressively.

One of the best examples of what children can learn about language can be seen on the videotape "Bones" from the *Teachers Teaching Writing* series (1984). The teacher, Margaret Grant, leads the children into a discussion about poems, drawing attention to the poem's structure, rhythm and rhyme, and the use of unusual and powerful words. In preparing children to write their own poems, Grant reviews several alternatives from which they may choose, saying the choice is theirs to make. The beauty of the video lies in its illustration of learning by exposure to a literary model. Led by a skillful teacher, the children discover that the power of poetry lies in its language and structure.

Another value of literature lies in its power to evoke emotions. Holdaway asserts that "works of the imagination . . . embody meanings which properly encompass both the emotions and those sensations which are subtle reminders of the organic functions which permeate all we do. For this reason, children's literature should constitute the central core of instructional programmes" (1979, 216). When children become engaged with a story, they often form an identification with aspects of the story that hold personal meaning for them. They often show personal reactions to a character or situation, relating such elements to their own lives. Because emotional reactions come naturally as children read, it is important for teachers to capitalize on oral and nonverbal responses, shaping and building other forms of expression, including writing. Diary and journal writing are particularly "safe" outlets for emotional responses to reading. Two second graders wrote these responses after hearing *Where the Wild Things Are* by Maurice Sendak (1973):

> Max's mother and father didn't know how to handle him. Sometimes he did bad things and only his friends in the jungle knew that he was good. It's nice to have good friends who know. *Cindy, Grade 2*

> If I was Max, I'd go back to the place with wild things. He's not gonna get his way at home anyway. Anyway, he needs some good friends. *Jim, Grade 2*

These reactions provide ample evidence that these youngsters possessed some insight into human needs. Both were able to convey their feelings in their spontaneous reactions, dictated to the fourth grader who read the story aloud.

One third grader wrote with sensitivity and insight after reading about sibling conflicts in Lillian Hoban's *No, No, Sammy Crow* (1981):

> I wished I didn't be so mean to my brother. He's just a kid and needs me. I guess I can walk him to school in the mornings.

Illustration from p. 13 of WHAT'S UNDER MY BED? by James Stevenson.
Illustration: Copyright © 1983 by James Stevenson. By permission of
Greenwillow Books, a division of William Morrow and Co., Inc.

A second-grade class developed a group story about things under their
beds after the teacher shared *What's Under My Bed* by James Stevenson
(1984). Children were eager to show emotion through words and
pictures as each child contributed a one-page part to the large bulletin
board display. Their works ranged from funny to scary, cuddly bears
to ugly monsters, and assorted surprises like fairies, pets, food, and
spaceships. Each illustration was accompanied by a written text that
described the reaction of the child looking under the bed.

Exposure to good literature also provides models of literary forms
to talk about and follow. Carefully led discussions of books will help
draw out the children's observations of the type and structure of
stories being read. Although formal study of literature is not appropriate at this level, children can discover and appreciate the inherent
characteristics of folktales, fables, fantasy, poetry, and realistic fiction.
As children mature in reading, they will sense the structure (narration,
description, cause and effect, etc.) of written materials and will adapt
their reading and responses accordingly. Children are naturally curious
and will want to experiment with their own writing, using familiar
stories as models for their creations. In addition to literary forms,
children should be encouraged to use other forms of writing. While
children are capable of writing in a variety of forms, they may need
some encouragement to explore approaches other than expression and
narration. The following may prove useful:

            rewriting endings   letters
            rewriting titles   author interviews

newspaper reviews	"book week" slogans
announcements	advertisements
designing bookjackets	group stories
mobiles	summaries
translations	dialogues

As children gain experience with various forms of literature, they can begin to develop their own stories and poems. In addition to creating pictures with paint, crayon, or collage, children may be guided to respond to literature through various forms of writing. A child may choose the one that best conveys his or her own personal response to the literary selection.

After reading poems about seasons, Sue Ann created her own collection, *A Handful of Poetry,* containing one poem for each season and "dedicated to people who enjoy poetry and simple illustrations." She cleverly added extra interest to her book by designing each page into a mitten. Sue Ann's work demonstrates a keen awareness of a literary form—poetry—and the total concept of creating a book that ties together title, illustrations, and design.

In addition to learning about type and structure, attention to the elements of good literature (setting, plot, characterization, theme, and style) may help students to become aware that authors employ different styles, adapting language to express individual ideas and purposes for writing. Although it is important for teachers to be knowledgeable about the elements of literature, that structural information should not be forced upon children. Such learning is gradual and may be encouraged by careful questioning and by exploring models of good writing. Elementary school children may be guided in their search for answers to such questions as:

1. When and where did the story take place?
2. What happens in the story?
3. Who are the characters in the story?
4. What happens to them?
5. How do they change?
6. What is the main idea of the story?
7. How does the author tell the story?

As children become accustomed to looking for these elements in what they read, they will eventually include them in their own writing. It is important to remember, however, that writing should be personal and meaningful, stemming from feelings and ideas within the child.

Imposing a particular structure or insisting that a story contain all of the elements of literature will result in artificial, stale, or stiff papers.

Colleen wrote and illustrated *The Fluffy Bunny* after reading *The Velveteen Rabbit.* Colleen's story is about Julie, who gets a big, fluffy, white toy bunny for Christmas. Julie enjoys showing her bunny to family and friends, but eventually goes outside to play, only to become seriously ill. The toys that kept her company during her illness need to be burned, according to the doctor. A beautiful fairy comes to the rescue, turning the toy into a real live bunny! Julie enjoys the bunny for a short time before it jumps off her lap and runs into the forest. Aware of the elements that make *The Velveteen Rabbit* an enjoyable story, Colleen includes setting, plot, characterization, and theme in her work. Her story of the love Julie has for her bunny resembles the use of a doll or toy often found in fantasy for children.

Using literature as a model or springboard for writing has at least one additional advantage. Children quickly discover that books come in different shapes and sizes; have a variety of page formats, print styles, and pictorial displays; and offer numerous organizational schemes. They are able to identify some features that many books have in common: table of contents, chapter indications, a title page, a dedication page, an index, endpapers, and bookjackets. They notice such phrases as "story by," "illustrated by," "story and pictures by," "the end," and "Once upon a time. . . ." These features of writing may be called the conventions of writing stories and books, and children quickly include such devices in their own works.

Sue Ann's poetry book included a dedication page and a table of contents. Colleen included the names of three friends who helped with illustrations. Kelly wrote *The Unhappy Leaf* and included front and end pages, each with illustrations of leaves. Both Joey and David wanted readers to know that theirs were award-winning books and included gold medals on the covers.

Suggestions for handling the conventions of writing can be found in children's books about writing. *A Writer* by M. B. Goffstein (1984) explains the process of being a writer. Susan Tchudi and Stephen Tchudi offer guidelines for the writing of stories and poems, as well as letters, journals, notes, and school papers, in *The Young Writer's Handbook* (1987). Two sources on book writing and publishing are Howard Greenfield's *Books: From Writer to Reader* (1976) and Harvey Weiss's *How to Make Your Own Books* (1974). Keeping a diary is found in *The Ramona Quimby Diary* by Beverly Cleary (1988). Although dated, *Someday You'll Write* by Elizabeth Yates (1962) and the *First*

Book of Creative Writing by Julia C. Mahon (1968) remain useful in illustrating the art and techniques of good writing.

Helping Children Write

It is important to be aware of several points when working with children who are developing writers.

First, teachers should not lose sight of the fact that most writing will consist of the child's own choice of subject matter, language, and style. Furthermore, authentic writing comes about only when the child has something to say for real reasons and when writing is an outgrowth of meaningful experiences (direct or vicarious). Ideas may come easily to children inspired by a captivating story, brilliant illustrations, or unusual page layouts. Others may need time to rehearse for writing: thinking, sketching, talking, drawing, and reading. Teachers need to explore alternatives with children, helping them to discover what they can write about and how they can get started. Children will turn to the classroom library for ideas, as well as to each other.

Second, although children will benefit from having a variety of stimulants and experiences from which their own ideas may develop, teachers should not establish rigid frameworks, standards, or courses of study that may restrict creativity and produce artificial and structured writing lessons. This is not to say that some aspects of writing cannot be taught to children. Most instruction will be individualized and incidental, using a child's own draft, questions, or problems as the basis for help and support. Some group teaching might be effective and efficient when a new idea or a problem's solution would benefit many. Calkins (1986, 165) says that children often "lack a sense of what good writing is like" and that teachers should not relinquish their identities, avoiding teaching at the risk of decreasing student ownership of their writing. A useful tip should be shared, a bit of instruction given; don't be afraid to teach.

It is essential that children be allowed ample time to read, to engage in prewriting activities—thinking, talking, planning, and sketching ideas—and to write and share their writing with others. An excellent way to provide a conducive atmosphere for reading and writing is to have a "Writer's Corner" which may be combined with a "Literature Center." Such a center, where children could come and go freely, might include:

Materials—books, stories, poems, pictures, idea cards, magazines, dictionaries, and other print and nonprint materials

Supplies—paper, pencils, pens, magic markers, boxes, tape, costumes, scissors, paste, and other craft items

Equipment—records, record player, cassette player and tapes, overhead projector, puppet theater, camera, microcomputer and word-processing software

Teachers may find the corner or center a good place to display editing charts for the checking of punctuation, capitalization, sentence structure, and spelling. Such charts can be reviewed by students individually, in peer editing groups, or with the teacher prior to producing their final products.

Third, children and teachers should view good literature as models and stimulants for developing sensitivity to the language and elements of literary writing and for generating new ideas. Technical aspects such as literary analysis and terminology, figurative language, poetic meter, and formal accuracy should not be emphasized with young children. Because a "writing program [that] is based on literature," says Stewig (1980, 9), "does not mean that teachers should attempt to dissect what they read with the children." He goes on to say that the purpose of using literature as a basis for writing is "to draw out from children their reactions to what they read rather than consciously implant in their minds large amounts of cognitive information." Personal enjoyment should not be overlooked as a major purpose of reading literature. Teachers will eventually become sensitive to the proper balance between too little and too much discussion.

Fourth, antiquated forms of book reporting that are not appropriate for children and do not adequately reflect the quality of reading experiences must be avoided. Most traditional book reports are inadequately prepared and do not reflect genuine, meaningful, and enjoyable encounters with literature. Students should be encouraged to share their reading in forms they can handle and at times that are appropriate. There are many alternative activities that encourage children to put their writing to use:

making books	recording on tapes
choral reading	painting, drawing
storytelling	putting words to music
dramatizing	finger plays, puppet plays
making filmstrips	flannelboard reports

collages	rhythm activities
dioramas	field trips
literature maps	

Forms of sharing that integrate reading with talking and writing will usually result in refreshing styles and products that not only indicate an awareness of the content of what was read initially, but will also demonstrate an interest in going beyond a text, allowing reading to come alive and be a part of personal experience. It is the teacher's responsibility to create a receptive climate for participating in such activities.

Receiving and Sharing

One author has suggested that "the way in which writing is received by the group when it is written may have more to do with encouraging the children to write than have the stimuli that are applied for this purpose" (Jones 1969). Moffett (1968, 192–94) agrees that the writer is influenced significantly by the responder(s). He contends that one reason for writing is to elicit certain reactions from a defined audience. Once a student completes a written product, therefore, it becomes important to identify a significant audience with whom the writing can be shared. Reactions to the composition and the feedback offered to the writer should be provided in the form of audience reception and response.

Implications for the classroom are apparent. Students should be encouraged to write for the interest and enjoyment of others, in addition to any personal writing they do for their own enjoyment. Writing of all kinds can be shared when the classroom environment is nonthreatening and informal. Although the teacher is obviously a significant adult audience, the students themselves are a more natural audience. With few exceptions, most writing is done to have others read it or hear it read. The reward of working through several drafts, revising and editing with the attendant reading these involve, is to share writing with classmates who know and appreciate the efforts put into a poem, story, or book. As Calkins (1986) describes, authors become "insiders" who are aware of what it takes to come up with an idea, develop it, modify it, and get it into a final product. Teachers and students help each young author to know and experience authorship and to see the authors behind what is read. She believes that the "reading-writing connections that matter most are the small 'ah-has' that happen when a youngster sees glimpses of the relatedness between reading and writing" (232).

Children should be encouraged to write for each other and to react to the writing of others in a discussion and workshop setting. This practice allows for talking, advising, reshaping, and sharing while work is in progress and soon after it is completed. Students may work in pairs or in small groups, exchanging papers, reading them, talking about improving their work—all in the context of learning in an interactive and supportive environment that encourages exploration of language, literature, and writing.

Role of the Teacher in a Workshop Setting

How children view the process of writing and the attitudes they develop toward it will be determined by the teacher. The role of the teacher in this type of workshop is clearly delineated.

First, as an interested reader, the teacher becomes an adult audience with whom writing is shared. At this point the teacher receives the child's writing and responds to the ideas and content in a sympathetic manner. The teacher encourages and motivates students to develop ideas and impressions in ways that appear appropriate to students' purposes for writing and that achieve the desired effects on the given audience. The teacher becomes a good listener who:

> encourages the student to read his or her draft aloud
>
> asks for the child's reaction to the writing (What do you like about this piece? What do you want to add? To change? Tell me more about this part.)
>
> responds positively to the child's comments and to the content of the writing by expressing an interest in the central idea and by asking questions that bring about revision possibilities
>
> focuses attention on the content and flow of the writing, keeping in mind the audience's need for information and clarification

Secondary to the teacher's role as an interested reader will be that of a coach and model who provides alternatives which may clarify or solve problems encountered during the various stages of writing. A workshop setting allows the teacher to assist children by consulting, responding, and coaching. Yatvin (1981) describes the teacher as one who moves about the room, helping children to shape their ideas, supplying spellings of words, offering solutions to problems, and suggesting ways to think about, develop, and expand ideas. A great deal of personal assistance can be given during individual writing conferences, in which a child shares a draft with an interested and enthusiastic teacher who elicits the kind of information that helps the child recognize things that would make the writing stronger. While the primary focus is on the purpose for writing and on content, discussion may eventually move to editing needs.

A third role of the teacher is to develop and expand the ability of children to respond to each other's writing and to offer suggestions for improving expression. If students are taught to teach each other, it would make possible "a lot more writing and a lot more response to the writing than a teacher could otherwise sponsor" (Moffett 1968, 196). Moffett views one's peers as a natural audience who can respond spontaneously to each other's writing. Suggestions for additions, deletions, and modifications may come from peer conferencing and teacher-guided group review sessions. Children can learn to:

> share their favorite part of a story
>
> explain how they felt when they read a story
>
> point to interesting or unusual words and phrases
>
> ask for clarification or needed information
>
> ask how the ideas for writing came about
>
> ask what the author will do next

Perhaps the most important goal for teachers is to help children become independent and to view evaluation as a matter of self-appraisal. The teacher's ability to ask questions may be the key to achieving this goal. During and after careful observations of the writing process, the teacher should encourage students to think about their own writing by asking appropriate questions. These may include:

> What do you like best about your story? Why?
>
> Is there anything you would like to change?
>
> Do you want to add something to your story?
>
> Where can you add words to help make a clear picture?
>
> Can you make the ending stronger?

Such questions should not seek specific "right" answers, but should aim to broaden or clarify the student's perception of the writing stimulus or the student's style of expression.

> [T]he purpose of this questioning is to develop habits of reflecting upon, thinking about, and reacting to written material. Each

child will develop this ability at his or her own level. Some will become very adept at it; others will have less success. The questioning does not become an end in itself but rather a means of encouraging this reflective attitude toward writing. (Stewig 1980, 234)

When children begin to see writing as an effective and satisfying means through which to communicate, they will find inner motivation to evaluate what they have written and will seek new forms of writing and more opportunities to read. In an ideal situation, students write for each other and read each other's writing, thereby making each writing activity a reading activity.

Conclusion

Getting children to write well and to develop a continuing enjoyment of writing are major goals of most teachers. Because literature develops a sensitivity to language, provides models for good writing, and serves as a springboard for many creative endeavors, one excellent way to develop active writers is to utilize the abundance of good literature as an impetus for personal writing. Since "reading [and especially reading fiction] affects one's way of talking and one's choice of topics, changes the perceptions of reality, of others and of the self, and influences attitudes and behavior" (Stahl 1975), then let reading lead to writing and writing lead to reading.

Recommended Books for Classroom Use

These books, cited as references throughout the chapter, are recommended for use in the classroom. Of course, there are many more titles that also are appropriate! An asterisk (*) denotes a title that is no longer in print.

Cleary, Beverly. 1988. *The Ramona Quimby Diary.* New York: William Morrow.

Goffstein, M. B. 1984. *A Writer.* New York: Harper.

*Greenfield, Howard. 1976. *Books: From Writer to Reader.* New York: Crown.

Hoban, Lillian. 1981. *No, No, Sammy Crow.* New York: Greenwillow Books.

*Mahon, Julia C. 1968. *First Book of Creative Writing.* New York: Franklin Watts.

Sendak, Maurice. 1973. *Where the Wild Things Are.* New York: Harper.

Stevenson, James. 1984. *What's Under My Bed.* New York: Puffin.

Tchudi, Susan, and Stephen Tchudi. 1987. *The Young Writer's Handbook.* New York: Aladdin.

*Weiss, Harvey. 1974. *How to Make Your Own Books.* New York: Crowell.

Williams, Margery. 1969. *The Velveteen Rabbit.* New York: Doubleday.

*Yates, Elizabeth. 1962. *Someday You'll Write.* New York: E. P. Dutton.

References

Atwell, Margaret A. 1980. The Evolution of Text: The Interrelationship of Reading and Writing in the Composing Process. Unpublished dissertation, Indiana University.

Atwell, Nancie. 1984. Writing and Reading Literature from the Inside Out. *Language Arts* 61 (3): 240–52.

Blount, Nathan. 1973. Research on Teaching Literature, Language and Composition. In *Second Handbook of Research on Teaching,* edited by Robert Travers. Chicago: Rand McNally.

"Bones." 1984. *Teachers Teaching Writing* series. Distributed by Association for Supervision and Curriculum Development and the National Council of Teachers of English.

Calkins, Lucy McCormick. 1986. *The Art of Teaching Writing.* Portsmouth, N.H.: Heinemann.

Clay, Marie M. 1975. *What Did I Write?* Portsmouth, N.H.: Heinemann.

DeFord, Diane E. 1981. Literacy: Reading, Writing and Other Essentials. *Language Arts* 58 (6): 652–58.

Dyson, Anne Haas. 1981. Oral Language: The Rooting System for Learning to Write. *Language Arts* 58 (7): 776–84.

Graves, Donald H. 1978. We Won't Let Them Write. *Language Arts* 55 (5): 635–40.

———. 1983. *Writing: Teachers and Children at Work.* Portsmouth, N.H.: Heinemann.

Holdaway, Don. 1979. *The Foundations of Literacy.* New York: Ashton Scholastic.

Hunter, Mollie. 1976. *Talent Is Not Enough: Mollie Hunter on Writing for Children.* New York: Harper and Row.

Jones, Anthony. 1969. Writing in the Primary and Middle School. *English in Education* 3 (3): 57–61.

King, Martha, and Victor Rentel. 1982. *The Transition to Writing: Cohesion and Story Structure.* Columbus, Ohio: The Ohio State University Research Foundation.

Moffett, James. 1968. *Teaching the Universe of Discourse.* New York: Houghton Mifflin.

National Assessment of Educational Progress. 1975. *Writing Mechanics, 1969–1974: A Capsule Description of Changes in Writing Mechanics.* Washington, D.C.: U.S. Government Printing Office.

————. 1981. *Reading, Thinking, and Writing.* Denver, Colo.: NAEP.

Rentel, Victor, and Martha King. 1983. Present at the Beginning. In *Research on Writing: Principles and Methods,* edited by Peter Mosenthal et al. New York: Longman.

Stahl, Abraham. 1975. Creative Writers on the Effects of Reading. *Journal of Reading Behavior* 7:111–22.

Stewig, John Warren. 1980. *Read to Write.* New York: Richard C. Owen.

Yatvin, Joanne. 1981. A Functional Writing Program. In *Perspectives on Writing in Grades 1–8,* edited by Shirley Haley-James. Urbana, Ill.: National Council of Teachers of English.

Related Readings

Calkins, Lucy McCormick. 1986. *The Art of Teaching Writing.* Portsmouth, N.H.: Heinemann.

This is certainly one of the most insightful, as well as enjoyable, books on the subject. Calkins presents an anecdotal discussion of her experiences with writing at various grade levels and for various purposes. She is masterful at tying together practice, theory, and research. Particularly useful are the sections on "How Children Change as Writers," "Writing Conferences," and "Reading-Writing Connections."

Newkirk, Thomas, and Nancie Atwell. 1982. *Understanding Writing: Ways of Observing, Learning and Teaching, K–8.* Chelmsford, Mass.: The Northeast Regional Exchange.

This collection of vignettes and reports by classroom teachers serves as an excellent example of how careful observations of skilled teachers have contributed to new insights about the process of writing and the practice of teaching writing. The sections on "Conferences" and "Writing and Reading" are particularly valuable.

Stewig, John Warren. 1980. *Read to Write.* New York: Richard C. Owen.

The entire premise of this book is using children's literature as a springboard for teaching writing. This is probably the most comprehensive resource on developing children's skills in writing fiction and poetry through a literature-based program.

6 Creative Drama and Story Comprehension

Mary Jett-Simpson
University of Wisconsin–Milwaukee

Mary Jett-Simpson suggests here that teachers are not confined to words, compositions, and illustrations in their efforts to develop literate children. Her alternative is an innovative use of creative drama to measure and develop comprehension. The approach moves drama, which has usually occupied only a peripheral place in the curriculum, into a more integral location in the language arts/reading program.

Jett-Simpson stresses drama as an aid to comprehension, and sets this emphasis in the context of a brief review of the major changes in comprehension writing and research of the last few years. She also focuses on the ways teachers may use drama to assess students' understanding of selections they have read. She gives examples of literature that can be used and ways those stories might be dramatized. Following her example, more teachers should be able to justify including drama as a means for enhancing comprehension.

"They roared their terrible roars and gnashed their terrible teeth . . . Let the rumpus begin." Children responding to these lines leap and turn, growl and look ferocious as they become wild things until Max finally tames them with a magic trick of staring straight into their eyes. Creative dramatization of *Where the Wild Things Are,* by Maurice Sendak, provides students with an opportunity to participate in the story and experience the excitement of stepping inside someone else's skin for a few moments—the ultimate comprehension of character. What are the educational benefits from such joyous activity for the language arts curriculum, specifically in connection with reading comprehension?

Unfortunately, creative drama is seldom thought of as a way of having children demonstrate and develop their reading comprehension. Rather, it is typically classified as something extra in the school curriculum—for fun and creativity after the "real" work of reading

91

class is complete: workbooks, oral reading, and answering literal questions. Usually, creative drama is placed in the curriculum "if there is time." The evidence, however, suggests that creative drama can be an appropriate activity for demonstrating comprehension.

Creative Drama Research

Educators have described at length the principles, values, and outcomes of creative drama experiences for children (Stewig 1983; Siks 1983; Wagner 1976). Although the research about its effects in the classroom is scanty, the general findings support the positive impact of creative drama on aspects of reading, including story comprehension (Pellegrini and Galda 1982; Galda 1982; Henderson and Shanker 1978), readiness (Yawkey 1980), vocabulary (Jiganti and Tindall 1986; Blank 1953; Pate 1977), and oral language (Vitz 1983; Stewig and McKee 1980). In a review of thirty-two creative drama studies, Vitz (1983) identified twenty-one where the results favored creative drama activities when teachers were trained in creative drama techniques. Dominant among these were oral language studies. Creative drama support of reading achievement wasn't found when reading achievement tests like the Iowa Test of Basic Skills (Bennett 1982) were administered. Such studies as Galda's (1982), however, found a positive relationship when using more sensitive measures of comprehension, specifically a criterion-referenced test and story retellings. Although the research is flawed in some of the studies and the results mixed (Stewig 1982), the general picture is that drama can support story comprehension, vocabulary, readiness, and oral language in certain circumstances.

Creative Drama and the Current View of the Reading Process

A strong case also can be made for selecting creative drama as a means for developing and demonstrating story comprehension, based on the current view of the reading process. Reading comprehension has been treated as a reproductive process, where it was assumed that comprehension was simply a matter of getting meaning from the pages. Currently, it is recognized that reading is a constructive process. Readers come to texts with networks of background knowledge stored in their minds and then construct meaning by using that knowledge in interaction with the text and what they perceive they should do with the text. Little or no meaning can be constructed if readers lack background knowledge about the selection. It is no longer thought that meaning resides on the page to be transferred into readers' heads (Pearson 1985).

A logical instructional conclusion, based on this view of the reading process, is that instruction should include high, active student involvement where children are encouraged to use strategies for activating background knowledge and constructing the meaning of the text. The nature of creative drama demands active construction of the meanings of stories. In order to dramatize, students must use their background knowledge in combination with text clues to build that meaning. The dramatization of vocabulary, parts of stories, and complete stories is a kind of paraphrase and informal retelling that results in a direct demonstration of story comprehension.

Creative Drama and Reading Comprehension: Partners in Constructing Meaning

Teachers typically limit their thinking about the role of creative drama to dramatizing an entire story after reading. However, creative drama can also be used flexibly in various forms throughout a reading comprehension experience.

Before Reading: Background Knowledge

The central role of background knowledge in reading comprehension is undeniable since it clearly shapes the comprehension of a selection. Attention should be given to activating and/or developing background knowledge prerequisites to reading a selection (Anderson and Pearson 1984). This is particularly crucial when the selection contains central concepts and themes that are partially or far removed from students' backgrounds or experiences. Creative drama can be an effective way to bridge from students' personal experiences to the key concepts and themes of a story, while acting as a motivation device for stimulating interest in reading the story as well.

In *The Relatives Came* (Rylant 1985), a key concept is "relatives." Most students will have experienced visits from relatives, but probably few will have had an Appalachian mountain experience quite like the one in the story, where a crowd of relatives visits. To bridge from their known personal experiences to the new experience of the book, students can discuss how they feel when their relatives come. From their discussions, they can develop vignettes showing what happens when relatives visit and become part of the activity in different rooms in their homes. After the story is read, discussion can focus on comparison and contrast of personal experiences with the one in the story.

During Reading: Vocabulary Dramatization

Developing the meaning of new vocabulary words can be enhanced by acting out a few key meanings as they arise in the context of stories (Jiganti and Tindall 1986).

Procedure

1. Before reading a selection aloud, teachers can identify several words or concepts central to the meaning of the story that are either different in meaning from students' life experiences, or are not clearly defined in the story context. Special attention should be given to action, descriptive, and emotion words which can be quickly and meaningfully communicated through drama.

2. When reading, the teacher can stop after the section where the unfamiliar word appears and invite the students to use the available story and life experience clues to its meaning.

3. Teachers clarify confusions of meaning by discussion and/or demonstration dramatization.

4. Teachers guide whole-group dramatization.

For example, in the timeless old story *Millions of Cats,* by Wanda Gag (1988), there is a section where the very old man's journey to find the cats is described.

> And he set out over the hills to look for one. He climbed over the sunny hills. He trudged through the cool valleys. He walked a long, long time and at last he came to a hill which was quite covered with cats.

Students will certainly understand *climbed* and *walked* from life experiences. They have probably all *trudged* as well but don't know the action by that label. Teachers can help students bridge from their personal experience to the new word through vocabulary dramatization. Students are likely to be able to identify that it is some kind of movement, sort of like walking. Teachers can then talk about an example from their own lives where they trudged, followed by a demonstration of the movement. "I can remember a time when I missed my bus and had to walk home. I was so tired by the end that I was trudging. I moved a lot like this." Students can talk about times they have trudged, followed by dramatizing the very old man's movements—first climbing the hills, then trudging the valleys, then walking—to show the contrast among the actions, experiencing how tired the man was becoming during his journey.

Shadow (Cendrars 1982), the Caldecott award-winning book illustrated by Marcia Brown, is full of words that invite dramatization of the shadow that, among other things, nestles, perches, soars, flops, and crashes.

During Reading: Inferential Comprehension—Prediction

Inferential comprehension requires readers to collect information from the page and combine it with their background knowledge—a process readers do naturally with varying degrees of effectiveness. Inference is necessary to comprehension of any piece, since there are always certain things authors expect readers to be able to fill in from experiences. This is a central ingredient of the contract between authors and readers. An important aspect of inferential comprehension is making predictions about what will happen in a story, then reading further to confirm or reject the predictions (Hansen 1981). Creative drama can be used effectively to support the prediction process. To do predictive dramatization, students must interpret what has occurred in the story in relationship to their background knowledge in order to build from those events to predict the next episode.

Procedure for Predictive Creative Drama

1. Before working with students, teachers read the story and identify episodes.
2. Teachers guide prediction of episodes, up to the one students will be dramatizing.
   a. Prediction: "What do you think will happen next? Why?" Teachers write predictions on board.
   b. Students read episode.
   c. Confirm, revise, or eliminate prediction: "Let's look over our predictions. Which ones shall we keep? Cross out? Change? Why?"
   d. Repeat the prediction process up to a key episode in the story.
3. Students form small groups to plan and develop a dramatization of what they think will happen next.
4. Each group dramatizes its prediction for the others.

5. Discussion of the likenesses and differences and the evidence for the prediction follows.

6. In the cliff-hanger style of old radio shows, the lesson for the day can be concluded at this point, leaving the students dangling.

7. The following day the book can be read so students can compare their dramatic predictions with the author's story decision.

Predictive creative drama would work well with Jane Yolen's *Sleeping Ugly* (1981), a humorous variation on the Sleeping Beauty fairytale. Teachers can have students do oral prediction and discussion for each episode up to the third wish, then form several dramatization groups to develop and act out predictions of the third wish episode. In the story, beautiful princess Miserella, who has a nasty disposition, gets lost in the woods where she meets an old fairy and eventually, orphaned Plain Jane. The fairy tells Plain Jane that she can have three wishes because of her considerate behavior toward the old fairy, which makes Miserella so furious that she stamps her foot angrily. The fairy tells Miserella to stop or she will turn the foot to stone; of course, Miserella doesn't, so her foot turns to stone. Plain Jane uses her first wish to return Miserella's foot to normal. ("What will happen next? Why?") When Miserella calls Plain Jane "stupid," the fairy makes frogs hop from her mouth. But Plain Jane uses her second wish to help Miserella again. One wish remains. At this point the teacher can stop reading and direct the students to form groups of three to do a dramatization predicting what Miserella, Plain Jane, and the old fairy will do in the third wish episode.

During Reading: Inferential Comprehension—Characterization

A strong feature of creative drama is that to dramatize characters effectively, students must begin to infer and interpret a character's thoughts, feelings, and actions in order to act the role. Drama can assist students in exploring characters more deeply. Piaget (1928) observed that students' interpretation of people begins with directly observable behaviors and gradually moves to understanding the psychological interior. The elementary school years are the major developmental period for students' abilities to "people read," that is, to understand their covert behaviors, feelings, attitudes, and motivations (Flavell 1970), with this ability becoming more accurate and refined over time. Gradually, students are able to interpret characters in a given situation from different points of view, which reflects the developmental behavior of decentering (Piaget 1928). Assuming the role of a character puts students inside the story, whereas scripted questions, typical of reading comprehension lessons, generally require students to stand outside the story as observers abstractly distancing themselves from the action. The concreteness of creative drama may be especially beneficial to students of seven to eleven years, whom Piaget (1928) identified as members of a concrete operational stage of development. Many teachers have had experiences with students of these ages who were limited in their ability to give verbal explanations, but who could demonstrate what they meant. A frequent comment from such a child is, "I can't tell you, but I can show you what I mean."

A simple procedure for beginning to guide students in taking on a character's role is the *dramatic interview.* Instead of asking questions such as, "What was the first little pig feeling when the wolf knocked on the door? Thinking? Planning to do?" etc., teachers can reframe questions into a character interview.

Procedure: Dramatic Character Interview

1. Teachers identify spots in the story where students' comprehension of character will be increased by assuming the role of the character. Interviews can be conducted during or after reading the story.
2. Teachers summarize the context of the situations at these points to set the scene for the interviews.
3. Teachers ask students to assume the roles of characters. Several students can dramatize the character at the same point as a basis for discussing different interpretations.

Dramatic character interviews would be a good warm-up for full dramatization of the trickster tales of Brer Rabbit and Brer Fox in Julius Lester's splendid retelling of *The Tales of Uncle Remus* (1987). Instead of asking scripted questions about "Brer Rabbit and the Tar Baby"—such as "What kind of character is Brer Fox? Brer Rabbit?"— teachers can reframe questions into character interviews. For example: "You are Brer Fox hiding in the bushes waiting for Brer Rabbit to come by and see Tar Baby. Mr. Fox, what are you feeling and thinking right now?" "You are Brer Rabbit stuck fast to Tar Baby and here comes Brer Fox. What are you thinking and feeling?"

Procedure: Dramatization of Character Change

Dramatization of character change, or lack of it, can focus students' attention on the relationship between the nature of characters and the impact of events on them as human beings in much greater depth than asking, "How did Sam change from the beginning to the end of the book?"

1. Teachers select a book where character change is central to the story.

2. Teachers provide students with a framework (see Figure 1) for mapping or charting character change during or after students' reading of the book. Three central episodes from the beginning, middle, and ending can provide the settings for tracking changes, or the focus can be more generally on the beginning, middle, and ending of the story. Students can be divided into three-member study groups for each character to be traced.

3. After students make their notes, each study group decides who will act out the character at the three different stages of development.

4. All groups discuss and plan how to put their characters together for the dramatization and rehearse their scenes, if desired.

5. Students enact the dramatization in the three scenes they traced for each character. Videotaping the sequence would be added motivation and also provide the means for reviewing the interpretations for discussion.

A finely crafted book for dramatizing how events in the lives of characters change their feelings, thoughts, beliefs, motivations, and

CHARACTER CHANGE NOTES FOR _____

Changes in: Story segments:	feelings	thoughts	beliefs	motivations	actions
Beginning					
Middle					
Ending					

Figure 1. Framework for mapping character change.

actions is the Colliers' book *My Brother Sam Is Dead* (1985), a Newbery honor book. The Revolutionary War provides the setting for the Meekers, an American family, in conflict over their varying points of view: patriot, Tory, pacifist, and uncertain. Three drama segments can be developed by having students divide into groups to develop character notes about Mr. Meeker, Mrs. Meeker, Tim, Sam, General Reed, and Betsy, looking for their positions on the war at its beginning, at the height of the fighting, and at the end of the book. Teachers can set the scene for the dramatization of each episode: "Imagine your characters all gathered around the kitchen table for the evening meal in the Meekers' house, discussing the war. You know your character well. How would he or she participate? What would he or she say? You are that character. Now everyone put yourself in the scene. 'Scene 1—War Discussion in the Meekers' Kitchen: In the beginning. . . .' " Scene-setting is repeated for subsequent episodes. Powerful comprehension insights can be gained from such a dramatization.

Although Doreen Rappaport provides less direct insight into the psychological interiors of characters, *Trouble at the Mines* (1987) could be used effectively with the procedure just described. Since much of the story is revealed through action and conversation, readers will be challenged to infer many of the characters' feelings, thoughts, beliefs, and motivations through close examination of their actions. The book is a natural choice to enrich social studies classes studying that era of American history when workers were striking for better wages and working conditions—in this case, in the coal mining town of Arnot, Pennsylvania, in 1898. The Wilson family becomes the focus for the effects of the conflict and strife caused by the strike. The influence of Mother Jones, an organizer for the United Mine Workers of America, is also seen throughout the story.

During Reading: Story Structure

The positive effects of knowledge about story structure on comprehending and recalling stories has been well documented (Bowman 1980; Fitzgerald and Spiegel 1983; Tierney and Cunningham 1984; Mandler and Johnson 1977; Stein and Glenn 1979). Simply discussing stories by using questions based on story structure (Beck et al. 1982) and using story structure to organize story recall and telling (Gordon and Braun 1982) and writing (Fitzgerald and Spiegel 1983) have been found to improve story comprehension.

Stories have organizational patterns and characteristics that reflect their culture. Common to Western culture is the goal-based story, where the basic structure consists of a setting, theme, plot, and resolution. The setting consists of characters, location, and time of story; theme is related to the main goal of the protagonist and the intended message of the author; plot contains episodes which can be subdivided further, depending on which model of story structure is used; and finally, the resolution, which reveals the outcome of the main character's goal. Although there is variation in the terms used to describe the episode sequence, the underlying concepts are the same for a goal-based narrative (Figure 2). Some event triggers the episode where the main character responds, then attempts to reach the goal, which results in an outcome. The episode structure answers the questions, "How did it start? What happened? How did it end? How did the next episode start?"

The episode structure of the goal-based story typically reflects a series of attempts by the main character to reach the goal. However, this is not always the case. In some instances, an episode embedded in a goal-based story may be a simple reaction to the initiating event of the episode. The Mandler and Johnson (1977) episode description

Stein and Glenn	Thorndyke	Mandler and Johnson
(1977)	(1977)	(1977)
Initiating event	Subgoal	Beginning
Internal response	Attempt	Development
Attempt	Outcome	simple reaction
Consequence		action
Reaction		(or)
		complex reaction
		goal path
		Attempt
		Outcome

Gordon	Fitzgerald and Spiegel
(1983)	(1983)
Complex Pattern	
Starter event	Beginning
Inner response	Reaction
Action	Goal
Reaction	Attempt
What happened	Outcome
Simple pattern	
Beginning	
Middle	
Ending	

Figure 2. Variations in descriptions of episode structure.

(Figure 3) provides for this variability by including both the simple reaction episode and the goal-based episode as options. Many Japanese folktales, which reflect the Buddhist value of not encouraging goal-oriented behavior, consist primarily of the simple reaction episode structure for the main character; however, the antagonists of these tales usually have a goal, which is typically to try to obtain the same luck as the protagonist (Matsuyama 1983). In working with story structure then, it is important to recognize and accommodate variability when it occurs by modifying and using story structure flexibly to describe the organizational patterns idiosyncratic to particular stories.

Teachers can map stories with their students by using a simple story map (Figure 3) or a more complex map, depending upon the needs of the students and the purpose of the lesson. Activities such as dramatic character interviews and predictive creative drama can be effectively included with story mapping. When the story map is created with children as they read, it provides a summary of the episodes, which can be used as a reference point for these activities.

The clear episodic structure of *It Could Always Be Worse* (Zemach 1986), for example, makes it especially strong for mapping and

Setting *Place:* a small village
Time: Once upon a time . . .
Main character: a poor unfortunate man
Problem It is too crowded and noisy in the one-room hut.
Goal To reduce the noise and crowded conditions.
Episode 1
Beginning: The poor man goes to the rabbi for advice.
Development: Rabbi tells him to put chickens, a rooster, and goose in the hut.
Outcome: The poor man follows the advice and life in the hut is worse than before.
Episode 2
Episode 2 is a repeat of Episode 1, except this time the rabbi says to add a goat.
Episode 3
Episode 3 is a repeat of one and two, except the rabbi says to add a cow.
Episode 4
Beginning: The poor man again asks for advice, saying home is like a nightmare.
Development: The rabbi tells him to remove the animals.
Outcome: The man follows the advice, resulting in peaceful sleep and plenty of room in the hut.
Resolution With just the family in the hut, it is a pleasure.
Theme Noise and crowded conditions are relative.
Figure 3. Simple Story Map for Margot Zemach's *It Could Always Be Worse.*

dramatization activities—the case for most traditional folk and fairy tales. As the story unfolds, the teacher and students can develop a story map. Dramatic character interviews with the "poor unfortunate man," after the teacher has read the beginning of the story where his goal and problem are established, could be conducted by saying, "Poor man, tell us about your problem and goal." It would also be interesting to interview his wife, his mother, and his six children who are also part of this household confined to a one-room hut. The charted elements can be used as a plan or guide for developing dramatizations of selected episodes or for discussing the story patterns, which give clues for predictive dramatization. After the goat episode, students will probably have identified the story pattern and quickly be able to infer that the poor man will make another attempt to solve his problem in a similar manner with a similar result. Using the episode structure established by Zemach, students can plan a dramatization that predicts the next episode. How will the poor unfortunate man begin his attempt? What will happen? What will be the outcome?

For younger children, *Hattie and the Fox* by Mem Fox (1988) is a good choice. A simple predictable story of Hattie the hen, who spots signs of danger in the bushes but is ignored by the rest of the barnyard animals when she brings the signs to their attention, would work well for a first story mapping experience combined with creative drama. Hazel's jealousy of her new baby brother monster is the theme in Pat Hutchins's humorous book *The Very Worst Monster* (1988), which young children will also be able to successfully map and enjoy dramatizing. The elegant new version of *Rumpelstiltskin*, by Paul Zelinsky (1986), will provide more of a challenge for middle-grade students.

After Reading: Storyboards and Story Structure

Reenactment of a complete story is an excellent way for students to retell or paraphrase (Morrow 1985), demonstrate knowledge of story structure (Fitzgerald and Spiegel 1983), and make inferences (Hansen 1981). The traditional scripted questions, based on taxonomies (Barrett 1968), typically tend to focus on fragments of a story and isolated bits of information, whereas the reenactment of a complete story requires students to orchestrate and integrate all elements of the story to construct its meaning as a whole. This is the realistic demand of story comprehension. To be complete, setting, character, plot, and theme must be present and interrelated. Creative drama forces attention on integration of these literary elements. Even when a particular character, as opposed to an entire story, is the focus of dramatization, the character cannot be dramatized without attention to plot. The story events involve the actions of the characters; these actions are the events of the story. The setting, which is the background for the action, contributes to the tone or mood of the scene. The scene taken as a whole helps build the meaning of the story.

Story structure can be used as the organizing framework for creative dramatization. An interesting way to approach the preparation can be through development of a story map in the form of storyboards. Storyboards are series of sketches used to plan and illustrate the composition and action of each camera shot in filmmaking (Mercer 1974; McClain 1978). A discussion or videotape of how movie or television producers, such as Steven Spielberg, use storyboard illustrations to plan scene composition and sequences in movie production could enhance the lesson.

Procedure: Storyboard Dramatizations

1. Teachers can direct the discussion of a story, helping students identify episodes.

2. The class can be divided into film director groups equal to the number of episodes.

3. Each group sketches storyboards for its episode to use as guides for planning the dramatization and videotaping of the episode.

4. Groups practice dramatizing their episodes.

5. Episode dramatizations are put together in a dramatization of the story as a whole.

6. A video camera is used to record the final production for enjoyment and further discussion.

Going to Squintum's (Westwood 1985) is a folktale with clear episodic structure for which students, in groups of four, could easily develop storyboards to guide their dramatizations for videotape production. The fox's goal is to maneuver the best dinner he can into his sack, and his problem is how to trick the people he meets into helping him. In the first episode, he leaves a bag containing a bumblebee with a woman, telling her not to look in the bag. She looks in the bag. The bee escapes and is eaten by her rooster. When the fox returns, he tells the woman that she must now give him the rooster, which she does, because her rooster ate the bee. The fox's first attempt is successful. Subsequent episodes follow the same structure until the final episode.

Wordless picture books are also an excellent source for dramatization. By buying two copies of a paperback wordless picture book, taking them apart, and laminating the pictures, the books become materials that can be used like storyboards.

Procedure: Wordless Picture Books as Storyboards

1. Teacher presents groups of students with mixed-up sets of pictures from several different wordless picture books.

2. Students work in their groups to develop a logical story sequence from the scrambled pictures. The process of producing an order will evoke a great deal of discussion about the story elements suggested by the pictures. To infer a meaningful sequence, students will find it necessary to focus carefully on picture details and discuss cause/effect relationships.

3. After the sequences are completed, the students can group the pictures by episodes.

4. The wordless picture book storyboards are used next to develop the dramatization.

5. On subsequent days, groups perform their dramatizations for each other.

6. A variation would be to have students work with one wordless picture book, dividing into small groups where each group works with one episode. In this case it will be necessary to agree on the names, occupations, and any other special features of the characters before doing the dramatization to assure story continuity.

Any wordless picture book with a clear story structure and interaction among characters will work well for the activity. Mercer Mayer's books in his frog series, many of which are available in paperback, would work well in the creative dramatic activity described. *Frog Goes to Dinner* (Mayer 1977), an especially delightful pictorial account of a frog who accompanies a family to a fancy restaurant for dinner, would be a good choice. Others that would be enjoyable to dramatize are *The Mystery of the Giant's Footprints* by Fernando Krahn (1977), *Alligator's Toothache* by Diane DeGroat (1977), *The Surprise Picnic* by John Goodall (1977), and *The Invitation* by Gabriel Lisowski (1980).

Procedure: Model Story Structure Used to Develop a New Story

Story structure can also be effectively used to develop a new story sequence for dramatization, based on the original story.

1. Teacher selects a story which has a clear story structure that students can use as a model for developing another story.
2. Students read and map story.
3. Students form writing teams and map a new story based on the original.
4. Students develop a dramatization of their new story to be presented to the class.

Jumanji (Van Allsburg 1981) ends with an open-ended challenge to readers' imaginations. In the story, the children played a board game called Jumanji, which they found in the park. The directions for the game emphasized the importance of reading and following directions precisely as stated. When the children played the game, each time they landed in a space what was written in the space came alive: for example, "lion attacks, move back two spaces" resulted in the appearance of a large, shaggy-maned lion who chased the boy through the house to the upstairs bedroom, where he plunged under the bed. When the lion tried to follow, he wedged his head under the bed, only to find himself stuck fast. Soon the house was full of animals and events from the game board. They would only disappear when someone reached the golden city at the game's end. At the end of the story, the children returned the game to its original position under a tree, only to see two other children snatch it and run across the park. They have recently heard these children described as children who never read directions—a perfect invitation to plan and dramatize *Jumanji II*, using the story structure pattern of *Jumanji*.

Creative Drama and Reading Comprehension: A Partnership Confirmed

Creative drama and reading comprehension are a natural partnership. It is impossible for students to do creative dramatization of stories without relating background knowledge to the story, interpreting characters, making inferences, considering cause/effect relationships, remembering the story line, and comprehending the story structure. It requires high, active involvement with the story—from the inside as participants, not from the outside as passive observers. The result is a joyous motivating experience in learning.

Recommended Books for Classroom Use

These children's books, cited as references in this chapter, provide good stories for creative dramatization. An asterisk (*) denotes that the title was out of print when this revised edition went to press.

Cendrars, B. 1982. *Shadow.* Translated and illustrated by Marcia Brown. New York: Scribner's.

Collier, C., and J. Collier. 1985. *My Brother Sam Is Dead.* New York: Four Winds.

*DeGroat, D. 1977. *Alligator's Toothache.* New York: Crown.

Fox, M. 1988. *Hattie and the Fox.* Illustrated by Patricia Mullins. New York: Bradbury.

Gag, W. 1988. *Millions of Cats.* New York: Putnam.

Goodall, J. 1977. *The Surprise Picnic.* New York: McElderry.

Hutchins, P. 1988. *The Very Worst Monster.* New York: Mulberry.

Krahn, F. 1977. *The Mystery of the Giant's Footprints.* New York: E. P. Dutton.

Lester, J. 1987. *The Tales of Uncle Remus.* Illustrated by Jerry Pinkney. New York: Dial.

Lisowski, G. 1980. *The Invitation.* New York: Harper and Row.

Mayer, M. 1977. *Frog Goes to Dinner.* New York: Dial.

Rappaport, D. 1987. *Trouble at the Mines.* New York: Crowell.

Rylant, C. 1985. *The Relatives Came.* Illustrated by Stephen Gammell. New York: Bradbury.

Van Allsburg, C. 1981. *Jumanji.* Boston: Houghton Mifflin.

Westwood, Jennifer. 1985. *Going to Squintum's: A Foxy Folktale.* New York: Dial.

Yolen, J. 1981. *Sleeping Ugly.* Illustrated by Diane Stanley. New York: Coward-McCann.

Zemach, M. 1986. *It Could Always Be Worse.* New York: Blue Ribbon.

Zelinsky, P. 1986. *Rumpelstiltskin.* New York: E. P. Dutton.

References

Anderson, R., and P. D. Pearson. 1984. A Schema-Theoretic View of Basic Processes in Reading. In *Handbook of Reading Research*, edited by P. D. Pearson, 255–91. New York: Longman.

Barrett, T. 1968. Taxonomy of Cognitive and Affective Dimensions of Reading Comprehension. Included in a chapter by T. Clymer in *The Sixty-Seventh Yearbook of the National Society for the Study of Education, Part 2*. Chicago: University of Chicago Press.

Beck, I., R. Omanson, and M. McKeown. 1982. An Instructional Redesign of Reading Lessons: Effects on Comprehension. *Reading Research Quarterly* 17:462–81.

Bennett, O. 1982. An Investigation into the Effects of Creative Experience in Drama upon the Creativity, Self-Concept and Achievement of Fifth and Sixth Graders. Doctoral dissertation, Georgia State University.

Blank, W. 1953. The Effectiveness of Creative Dramatics in Developing Voice, Vocabulary, and Personality in the Primary Grades. Doctoral dissertation, University of Denver. In *Doctoral Dissertations Accepted by American Universities 1952–1953* 20:269.

Bowman, M. 1980. The Effect of Story Structure Questioning upon the Comprehension and Metacognitive Awareness of Sixth Grade Students. Doctoral dissertation, University of Maryland. In *Dissertation Abstracts International* 42:626A.

Dreher, M., and H. Singer. 1980. Story Grammar Instruction Unnecessary for Intermediate Grade Students. *The Reading Teacher* 34:261–68.

Flavell, J. 1970. Concept Development. In *Carmichael's Manual of Child Psychology*, edited by Paul Mussen, 983–1,059. New York: John Wiley and Sons.

Fitzgerald, J., and D. Spiegel. 1983. Enhancing Students' Reading Comprehension through Instruction in Narrative Structure. *Journal of Reading Behavior* 17 (2): 1–17.

Galda, L. 1982. Playing about a Story: Its Impact on Comprehension. *The Reading Teacher* 36 (1): 52–55.

Gordon, C. 1982. *Improving Reading Comprehension and Writing: The Story Grammar Approach*. Calgary, Canada: Braun and Braun.

Gordon, C., and C. Braun. 1982. Story Schemata: Metatextual Aid to Reading and Writing. In *New Inquiries in Reading Research and Instruction*, edited by J. Niles and L. Harris, 262–68. Rochester, N.Y.: National Reading Conference.

Hansen, J. 1981. The Effects of Inference Training and Practice on Young Students' Reading Comprehension. *Reading Research Quarterly* 16:391–417.

Henderson, L. C., and J. L. Shanker. 1978. The Use of Interpretive Dramatics Versus Basal Reader Workbooks for Developing Comprehension Skills. *Reading World* 17:239–43.

Jiganti, M. A., and M. Tindall. 1986. An Interactive Approach to Teaching Vocabulary. *Reading Teacher* 39 (5): 444–48.

McClain, B. 1978. *Super 8 Film-Making from Scratch*. Englewood Cliffs, N.J.: Prentice-Hall.

Mandler, M., and N. Johnson. 1977. Remembrance of Things Parsed: Story Structure and Recall. *Cognitive Psychology* 9:111–51.

Matsuyama, U. 1983. Can Story Grammar Speak Japanese? *The Reading Teacher* 36 (7): 666–69.

Mercer, J. 1974. *An Introduction to Cinematography.* Champaign, Ill.: Stipes.

Morrow, L. 1985. Retelling Stories: A Strategy for Improving Young Students' Comprehension Concept of Story Structure and Oral Language Complexity. *Elementary School Journal* 85:647–61.

Pate, T. 1977. An Investigation of the Effects of Creative Drama upon Reading Ability, Verbal Growth, Vocabulary Development, and Self-concept of Secondary School Students. Dissertation, East Texas State University. *Dissertation Abstracts International* 38:6506A.

Pearson, P. D. 1985. Changing the Face of Reading Comprehension Instruction. *The Reading Teacher* 36 (8): 724–38.

Pellegrini, A. D., and L. Galda. 1982. The Effects of Thematic-Fantasy Play Training on the Development of Students' Story Comprehension. *American Educational Research Journal* 19:443–52.

Piaget, J. 1928. *Judgment and Reasoning in the Child.* New York: Harcourt Brace.

Siks, G. B. 1983. *Drama with Children.* New York: Harper and Row.

Stein, N., and C. Glenn. 1979. An Analysis of Story Comprehension in Elementary School Children. In *Advances in Discourse Processes: New Directions in Discourse Procession,* vol. 2, edited by R. O. Freedle. Norwood, N.J.: Ablex.

Stewig, J. W. 1982. Dramatic Arts Education. In *Encyclopedia of Educational Research,* 460–64. New York: Macmillan.

———. 1983. *Informal Drama in the Elementary Language Arts Program.* New York: Teachers College Press.

Stewig, J. W., and J. McKee. 1980. Creative Drama and Language Growth. *Children's Theatre Review* 29 (3): 1, 14.

Thorndyke, P. 1977. Cognitive Structure in Comprehension and Memory of Narrative Discourse. *Cognitive Psychology* 9:77–110.

Tierney, R., and J. Cunningham. 1984. Research on Teaching Reading Comprehension. In *Handbook of Reading Research,* edited by P. D. Pearson, 609–55. New York: Longman.

Vitz, K. 1983. A Review of Empirical Research in Drama and Language. *Children's Theatre Review* 32 (4): 17–25.

Wagner, B. J. 1976. *Dorothy Heathcote: Drama as a Learning Medium.* Washington, D.C.: National Education Association.

Yawkey, T. 1980. Effects of Social Relationships Curricula and Sex Differences on Reading and Imaginativeness in Young Students. *Alberta Journal of Educational Research* 26:159–68.

Related Readings

Cottrell, J. 1987. *Creative Drama in the Classroom, Grades 4–6.* Lincolnwood, Ill.: National Textbook.

Following an introductory chapter that describes the relationship of creative drama to the language arts and learning theory, Cottrell discusses the roles of teachers in creating a climate for drama, planning for success, organizing and managing drama activities, and using leadership strategies to guide dramatization. Basic and advanced creative drama skills are presented, along with a chapter that should be of special interest to intermediate-grade teachers, integrating drama with the content areas. The appendixes will be a useful resource for additional references on creative drama and films, anthologies, poetry, and stories for use in dramatization. The final summary list of the activities and ideas, with page numbers for easy location, is a handy reference for teachers.

Elementary Drama Ad Hoc Curriculum Committee. 1985. *Elementary Drama Curriculum Guide.* Edmonton, Alberta: Ministry of Education.

Readers looking for a concrete example of a fully developed drama program for elementary schools will be delighted with this curriculum, available from Alberta Education.

McCaslin, N. 1987. *Creative Drama in the Primary Grades: A Handbook for Teachers.* New York: Longman.

McCaslin organizes her book in a creative drama developmental sequence, beginning with activities that focus on expressive use of the body and voice—including rhythmic and imitative movement, sensory awareness, pantomime, imaginative movement, and improvisations. These activities provide the foundation for creative dramatization of stories, poetry, and doing puppet shows. An extensive annotated bibliography of additional book, prose, poetry, film, and music references is included, along with several sample lesson plans. The summary of activities at the beginning of the book will help the teacher quickly locate those of greatest interest.

Manna, Anthony, editor. 1985. Drama and Language: Learning in Action. *English Language Arts Bulletin* 26 (2). Ohio Council of Teachers of English Language Arts.

This thematic edition of the bulletin provides readers with a number of articles that demonstrate the educational values of creative drama in learning and expression.

Thomas, S., and S. Dinges. 1986. *Curtain I: A Guide to Creative Drama for Children 5–8 Years Old.* New York: Trillium Press.

————. 1986. *Curtain II: A Guide to Creative Drama for Children 9–12 Years Old.* New York: Trillium Press.

Both collections of drama activities, when used in the context of a carefully developed drama program, will be a welcome resource for classroom teachers.

7 Literature across the Curriculum

Sam Leaton Sebesta
University of Washington

This chapter contrasts and compares tradebooks and textbooks. Sam Leaton Sebesta argues that tradebooks (fiction and non-fiction) often provide a stronger link between readers' experiences and a curricular topic than do textbooks. While tradebooks may not attempt comprehensive coverage of a topic, as textbooks do, they may often motivate and enlighten readers through engagement/involvement and elaboration.

Tradebook examples from each curricular area are presented, along with sources for locating good tradebooks pertaining to almost any topic. The chapter includes a discussion of questions, issues, and applications concerning the use of tradebooks in subject-area teaching, as opposed to presenting "a closed corpus of knowledge locked into a textbook."

British raiders have murdered Hannah, the deaf-mute pigkeeper. Until now the people of Okracoke, where Hannah lived, have ignored the war far away to the north of this little island off the coast of the Carolinas. Now they vow revenge. They'll send salt and other crucial supplies up the coast, past the enemy to Valley Forge, where General George Washington waits out the ugly winter with his fast-depleting Continental Army. Thus the distant war becomes *George Midgett's War* (Edwards 1985), for fourteen-year-old George and his father must make the delivery, a 300-mile trek by wagon and barge.

What does George Midgett learn during the journey? He learns that during war, injustice doesn't choose sides: the life-saving Croatan Indian guide is shot by patriots, not the British. He learns that there are many sides to the Revolution, not just the pro and con. He learns how greatly his own life is shaped by forces outside his own wishes and needs—forces that, in retrospect, people call history. Oh, so much he learns!

What do *we* learn? If our concept of history has been confined to a textbook summary of events, we learn here that history also contains a panorama of fully rounded characters whose existence is important and interesting. Literature, especially the historical novel, tells us that despite their anonymity, these people are not quite forgotten. It reminds us, too, of our own connections to the past. Given a small shift in time and place, we could have been with George Midgett on that barge. We could have heard the patriots argue against the war, some in the spirit of saving the colonies and some just to save their own pocketbooks and skins. In a sense, we *have* accompanied George on this journey and learned with him and beyond him.

When Janet Hickman reviewed *George Midgett's War* in her column, she concluded: "This is a novel that will carry readers with it on the personal and emotional level, but it also raises moral and social issues to be discussed in a study of the Revolution" (1986, 86). It is an exciting prospect—to use tradebooks containing a literary work such as this one so centrally in the curriculum. Let us examine some of its implications.

The Role of Tradebooks: A Social Studies Example

First, let's make some distinctions: tradebooks are not textbooks. Tradebooks are not designed to cover a body of knowledge whose parameters are defined by curricula. *George Midgett's War*, for example, is not a history of the American Revolution nor a description of the winter at Valley Forge. A textbook covering this period probably would present such a history and description. Tradebooks are less likely to be restricted by the various well-publicized taboos placed on textbooks by curriculum adoption committees and pressure groups. In a tradebook such as Milton Meltzer's *The American Revolutionaries* (1987), journals and letters of the colonists are not screened to eliminate graphic information about child abuse, disobedience toward parents, and carnage. In style and register, tradebooks run a full gamut of tone and genre, while textbooks are generally serious and expository. The romance of *Touchmark* (Lawrence 1975) or the suspense of *Rebecca's War* (Finlayson 1972) are not likely to be matched in textbook chapters about the Revolution.

Textbooks are more often assigned and studied "for learning," while tradebooks are more often self-selected by their readers and are read "for fun." This distinction parallels, respectively, Rosenblatt's efferent and aesthetic conditions of the transactional experience (1968). But it is this distinction that may lead to confusion in a classroom that diligently separates "reading to learn" from "reading for fun."

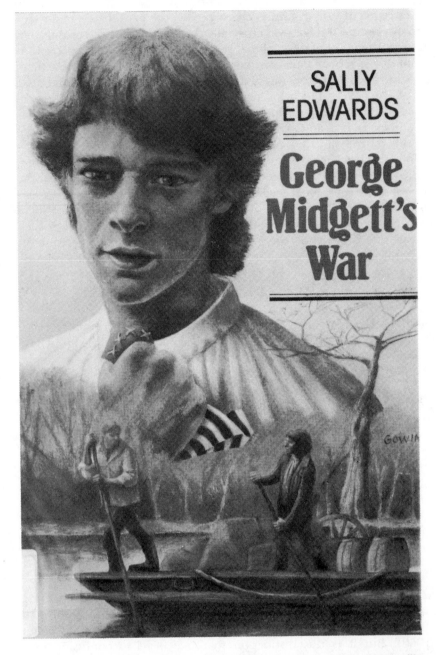

Reprinted by permission of Charles Scribner's Sons, an imprint of Macmillan Publishing Company from the cover illustration by Toby Gowing from GEORGE MIDGETT'S WAR by Sally Edwards. Copyright © 1985 Sally Edwards.

Suppose that a class of fifth graders is indeed studying the American Revolution. The teacher presents background information for the text chapter, the students read the chapter carefully, the class works together to "map" the chapter's contents, and there follows a fluent discussion led wisely from literal to inferential to interpretive levels. All seems well, and a test based more-or-less directly on the textbook chapter might indicate pleasing results. Mission accomplished.

Or is it? What about those "moral and social issues" that Hickman mentions? Did some patriots really oppose Washington and the Continental Army? Why the dreadful winter at Valley Forge anyway— why wasn't the army more comfortably housed in nearby Philadelphia? What was it *really* like to live in one of the colonies in 1777? What sort of "moral and social issues" were in the heads of all sorts of people—from the George Midgetts to the George Washingtons?

Who is to say that these are not important questions? And who is to assert that reading to find the answers to them is efferent reading "to learn" and not aesthetic reading "for fun"? As Woolsey and Burton (1986) point out in their study of intermediate graders' literary experience, "the same text can be read either efferently or aesthetically" (273). In the instance described here, we may hope that both purposes are served simultaneously. Certainly tradebooks, as opposed to textbooks, enable readers to achieve this enriched duality of purposes in their experience.

Tradebooks, then, when they pertain to a curricular topic, may bridge the gap between efferent and aesthetic reading related to the content areas. One social studies authority puts the matter this way: "An interesting story, literary selection, or incident can be used in the social studies to help formulate questions that are complete, precise, and testable" (Banks and Clegg 1985, 59). The observation holds true for other curricular areas as well—science, mathematics, and the humanities. In addition, literature can help answer such questions, bringing concomitant interest and satisfaction.

Tradebooks in Science, Mathematics, and the Humanities

Begin with a search for tradebooks relevant to a curricular topic, a kind of scavenger hunt whose participants include students, the teacher, the librarian, and other interested parties. It's a browsing expedition to bring back materials to arouse curiosity or to satisfy it. The search cuts across genres and levels of readability. It accommodates the wide variety of prior knowledge that students bring to any topic (Holmes and Roser 1987).

For example, a science unit on seas and oceans might begin with the shared discovery of Rhoda Blumberg's *The First Travel Guide to the Bottom of the Sea* (1983), with its opening gambit: "You will experience close encounters of a thousand kinds." The hypothetical journey is futuristic, but the panorama at the bottom of the sea is factual, even the lineup of fish waiting their turn for the services of a fish doctor! One may argue that such a book presents exotic information rather than what an oceanographer might deem essential. But *curiosity is essential* if most students are to get anywhere beneath the surface. This book, then, serves a worthy purpose.

Still tantalizing, but more intent upon revealing the sea as an ecosystem, are three books one might turn to next. *The World beneath the Sea* (Harris 1979) is brief (forty-eight pages) with easy readability, but it never waters down its watery information. Diagrams show ocean currents and food chains. Neap tides and spring tides, echo sounders, and sealabs are presented—not superficially but with plain respect for the reader's intelligence and curiosity. *Water World* (Settle 1984) addresses readers directly, asking them to join the search for a living fossil, for a food chain *not* derived from energy from the sun, and for truth versus tall tales throughout history—from the dolphins on Mycenaean vases to the elaborate quest of Cousteau. *Exploring the Sea: Oceanography Today* (Blair 1986) is, in fewer than a hundred pages, a compendium of sea information arranged under brief topics and with an extensive, clear index: a book for browsing but also for answering a reader's questions. More? Tradebooks serendipitous to a curricular topic can make the difference between a passive reader who quits when the bell rings and an active, lifelong, self-motivated reader/learner. Two-thirds of *Sharks, the Super Fish* (Sattler 1985) is glossary. If you doubt that anyone can devour a glossary, try this one on a reader fascinated by sharks. And even the less enthusiastic sea-goer will be interested to know that "there are more than three hundred kinds of sharks. Only thirty of these types have ever attacked humans." (I suppose the motto is that if you swim in sharky waters, take along your glossary.) The best thing about *Where the Waves Break: Life at the Edge of the Sea* (Malnig 1987) is that the color photos *exactly* match the text. When you read about suction cups and the eyespots on a starfish, you have a magnified picture right there so you can see. *Dolphins: Our Friends in the Sea* (Rinard 1986), published by the National Geographic Society, offers interviews with trainers and scholars, vivid color photos, and legends of dolphin heroics.

I've chosen to illustrate the contribution of tradebooks to the science curriculum by discussing one armful of books devoted to one broad science topic. This could be done with any science topic, by selecting books, by browsing, or by using some of the sources mentioned later in this chapter. The situation in mathematics is similar but different. There are books about specific curricular topics—set theory, areas and perimeters, adding fractions—but these are overshadowed by books of a more general nature, seeking to explain fundamental mathematics concepts and to make these concepts interesting.

"Counting books," dealing with cardinal numbers, are often wildly attractive, hence motivating. A simple one, such as Sara Lynn's *1 2 3* (1986), presents a numeral accompanied by corresponding dots and animal shapes to be counted. At the end, there's a panorama: the child is to identify sets of animals and count them. *Demi's Count the Animals One Two Three* (1986) is more sophisticated in every way, although the "counting" objective is the same. This time, the child is urged to count by twos and fives, and the sets of animals in the final panorama go spinning off the page.

Tradebooks clarify math concepts, often linking a reader's experience to an otherwise distant school topic. Thus, *666 Jellybeans! All That?* (Weiss 1976) contrasts arithmetic and algebra: "In algebra, you don't have to know what all the numbers are to begin with." Patricia Lauber's *The Story of Numbers* (1961), despite its older publication date, continues to prove to reluctant young mathematicians that numbers have, throughout history, aided people to record the past and to plan ahead. *How Much Is a Million?* (Schwartz 1987) wins admiration by showing exactly 100,000 stars and the computation that it will take you ninety-five years to count to a billion! These books build an efferent-aesthetic foundation for the mathematics curriculum.

Few modern textbooks for children treat the humanities: visual arts, drama, and music. Here, tradebooks help meet a basic need for aesthetic fulfillment and for self-realization through creative performance. Not everyone can respond to an extensive art history such as that presented in *Great Painters* by Piero Ventura (1984); or to great artists discussed in brief, memorable sketches as in *An Artists Album* (Goffstein 1985); or to an impressionistic narrative about colors in *Artists' Helpers Enjoy the Evenings* (Goffstein 1987). But an enthusiastic teacher or visiting artist can help engender interest through these books, sometimes introducing a lifetime of art appreciation. Paintings connected through story may be more accessible, as in

Thomas Locker's *Sailing with the Wind* (1986) and Jörg Müller's unique blend of drama, music, and painting in a book rendition of *Peter and the Wolf* (Prokofiev 1986).

Books to help children produce art are numerous, enticing, and more fulfilling than the outcome when students are merely directed to "draw something." *Draw 50 Cars, Trucks, and Motorcycles* (Ames 1986) is a primer on sketching, guaranteed to help a novice artist learn how to begin. *Easy Origami* (Nakano 1986) combines direction-following with the satisfaction of producing an admirable art product. *The Metropolitan Museum of Art Activity Book* (Brown 1983) shows how to make replicas of antique board games, Pantins (jumping dolls), stained glass windows, flip books, and tapestries—a not-to-be-missed combination of fine art appreciation and performance. And, if these and others fail to inspire art projects, try the directions for three-dimensional cosmic centipedes, a lunar colony computer, a meteor man, and an orbital ray detector, all provided in *Far Out: How to Create Your Own Star World* (West 1987).

Elsewhere I've discussed tradebooks presenting drama and music (Sebesta 1987). The point to be made here is that tradebooks on these topics are requisite to entering the world of the humanities, basic to the health of the spirit.

Questions about Using Tradebooks

Given thick textbooks and a tight schedule, a teacher might find the case for incorporating tradebooks centrally into the curriculum interesting but unworkable. Here are some questions one might ask, and some attempts at answering.

Is This Another "Add-on"?

The question might continue this way: "I have a set of objectives and required content in social studies, math, science, and all the rest. I have texts, manuals, worksheets, and tests. I have a specified amount of time. I will consider an 'instead of'—for instance, teaching a unit on national heroes instead of national holidays. But don't ask me to do an 'add on'—to add a group of tradebooks to what I'm already expected to cover."

One answer comes from the reading experts, who point out that fluent reading is a most sought-after goal of literacy. They note that fluency, developed only through practice, is neglected in many schools' reading programs. They cite evidence that voluntary reading by students in this nation is scant, an average of from zero to four minutes per day, depending on the group surveyed (Anderson et al. 1985, 77). To develop fluency and to increase voluntary reading are goals not to be ignored. They cannot be considered subordinate to the content goals of acquiring information. When it comes to necessary "instead of's" in education, wider reading of tradebooks deserves priority. Some experts believe that the resulting rise in fluency will more than compensate for reduced "on task" time spent on textbooks.

Another answer is that content instruction confined to direct teaching of a closed corpus of knowledge locked into a textbook has not, in the long run, proved itself—even when measurement is done through achievement tests alone, excluding other measures better designed to assess inquiry ability and attitude. (See, for some evidence, the five lead articles in *The Elementary School Journal*, November 1986, vol. 87, number 2.) A teacher or entire school might confidently do action research (Burton 1986) to find out whether an "instead of" approach that places tradebooks into the curriculum will equal or surpass more textbook-centered instruction.

Would I Need Thirty-two Copies?

No. The intent is not that every student read the same book, certainly not at the same time. The range of reading abilities precludes this, and so does the variety of interests. Ideally, we'd begin with a cluster of content-related tradebooks such as those mentioned in the preceding discussion, as varied in reading level and genre as possible.

Let's return to the Valley Forge example. *Buttons for General Washington* (Roop and Roop 1987) is quick and simple, compared to *George Midgett's War*. It's a spy story based on fact, about a Quaker boy named John Darragh who carried coded messages hidden in a button on his coat. He must get by the British guards in Philadelphia to travel the thirty miles to Valley Forge. But he hasn't gone far before he discovers that the button is missing, and when he slips back to the city he finds the button—in the hands of a British soldier! In addition to suspense, the book presents a you-are-there feeling for Philadelphia and Valley Forge at the time of the Revolution, contributing a feeling for history.

George Washington and the Birth of Our Nation (Meltzer 1986) reveals that during the winter of 1777, nearly half the colonists opposed the Revolution. General Washington wrote in a private letter that "no consideration upon this earth should have induced me to accept this command." The biography tells of a human side to Washington, who loved to dance and who named his horses Truelove and Sweetlips. It is not the stern portrait at the front of the schoolroom or in many textbooks.

Add two well-established novels of the Revolution: *Johnny Tremain* (Forbes 1981) and *My Brother Sam Is Dead* (Collier and Collier 1985). Add two of the easy, vivid biographies by Jean Fritz: *And Then What Happened, Paul Revere?* (1973) and *Can't You Make Them Behave, King George?* (1982). This is only a beginning. Note that in the 1987 edition of the *Subject Guide to Children's Books in Print,* a total of 47,540 titles are listed, arranged under 6,500 subject headings. The list does not include some notable out-of-print titles that can still be ferreted out of good libraries—for example, Marguerite Henry's droll tale of George Washington's encounter with *Cinnabar, the One O'Clock Fox* (1956).

For a class of, say, thirty-two students we need at least thirty-two tradebooks on our topic—but they should not be the same book. Even better, we might follow the recommendation of individualized reading proponents and ask for three books per student on our topic (Veatch 1968). Let these include single copies, double copies, a packet of five identical paperbacks to be read together by an interest group.

How Do I Get the Books?

Availability varies from school to school. My public library allows me to check out twenty-five books on a topic for one month if I convince the librarians that I need them for a classroom activity. In a nearby district, teachers collect books on a curricular topic into heavy cardboard file boxes to be passed from school to school. They're drawn from everywhere—from on-site purchases during vacations, parent groups, principals' discretionary fund purchases, and from me! The collection need not be a big one to get started. Sometimes a single addition makes a big difference in interest, as it did when we added *Susanna of the Alamo: A True Story* (Jakes 1986) to a meager collection on Texas history.

Availability of tradebooks is often a less serious problem than quality. A pretty cover cannot for long disguise a dull or inaccurate text. Using what she called a "Yawn Index," Betza (1987) evaluated books about computers and found that a majority of them fall short of appeal and utility; it took a long search to discover, for example, the valuable "Looking at Computer" series (Holland 1986).

How, Then, Do We Get a Quality Collection?

We browse, we share our enthusiasm—word of mouth still seems to be a good means of quality control! We consult librarians, who point out standard sources of reviews. *Best Books for Children* (Gillespie and Gilbert 1985), with 11,000 titles arranged by topic, is a compilation selected on the basis of reviews. *Appraisal—Science Books for Young People,* published four times a year, uniquely contains side-by-side critical reviews by scientists who read for accuracy and by educators who read for child appeal. Tradebooks relating to social studies are reviewed extensively each year in *Social Education,* while math trade-book reviews appear in most issues of *Arithmetic Teacher.* The "Book Selection Aids" appendix in *Children and Books* (Sutherland and Arbuthnot 1986, 666–71) presents an annotated list of review sources.

What about Controversial Books?

The Return of the Indian (Banks 1988), like its predecessor *The Indian in the Cupboard* (Banks 1988), may be said to contain unfavorable stereotypes of Native Americans. The stereotypes are intrinsic to both books' themes, for the books tell how Omri, the protagonist, learns that the stereotypes are false. Through Omri's eyes, we watch the transition from flat character to rounded character—not just of Little Bear and Bright Stars, the Indian couple, but of Boone the cowboy. Thus, both books are about the breaking down of stereotypes, the opposite of reinforcement of stereotypes. The books are popular. Their themes are developed through the working of plot and character, not didactic.

In some districts, books such as these are considered controversial. With what seems to me to be justified concern, some adults point out the stereotypic terms and behaviors. But no one should form an opinion about a book without first reading it all the way through. Usually the critics who begin by attacking *The Return of the Indian* are convinced, after reading and discussion, that it is a positive force against stereotyping. They suggest that a discussion guide, prepared for the student and the teacher, may be needed.

Controversy is also aroused by alleged lack of accuracy. One adult objected to the endnotes in *Socrates and the Three Little Pigs* (Mori 1986) because, she said, this "simple" mathematical presentation of combinatorial analysis omits vital information. Another objected to *Guinea Pigs Don't Read Books* (Bare 1985) because of what he considered to be a misstatement about the sounds emitted by these animals. And there are controversies derived on the basis of taste. An art teacher disapproved of the cartooned, farcical treatment of great artists in *Rembrandt Takes a Walk* (Strand 1986).

What's to be done? One alternative is to permit no tradebooks in the class except those that have been declared by some board or other to be absolutely free of controversy! Another alternative is to state a policy something like this:

> Tradebooks for this class are selected for quality, many of them for pertinence to the curriculum. They do not ignore controversy but attempt, instead, to handle controversy with fairness and accuracy. We discuss books openly, and we attempt to evaluate them with students. We teach an open, inquiring attitude, and we do not teach that authors' messages are irrefutable. Authors are fallible, like the rest of us, but we attempt to select those who are thoughtful and knowledgeable.

In addition to these ideas about controversial books, readers interested in this topic might want to read Davis (1979) who presents eighteen chapters written by experts on this topic, addressing a variety of issues related to censorship.

Ideas for Application

Before a unit begins, tradebooks about the topic are sought. Students are encouraged to browse and select. Above all, they are urged to tell about their discoveries and to assist in making a book display with captions to entice new readers. They may participate in a "talk show" to share their finds. Such interaction about literature among peers and between teachers and students was found by Southgate and her associates (1981) to be a crucial activity in successful reading programs.

One primary teacher, Utako Matsuyama, uses the shoebox approach. As pupils discover books that relate to what is to be studied, each puts the materials upright in a shoebox brought from home, placed along one wall and marked with the pupil's name. The shoebox becomes a miniature library, containing the selections that are considered most interesting and valuable by the pupil. When the class gathers to work on the topic (whether science, math, social studies, art, or music), students bring their shoeboxes. As a whole or in subgroups, they interact—reading aloud an important passage, explaining diagrams and maps, or demonstrating a process such as the complicated working of *Train* (Marshall and Bradley 1986), a book that neatly combines direction-following with technical information about mechanics.

As a unit gets under way, the teacher must ask: "Shall I teach emergently or shall I teach the content as the textbook presents its?" The "right" answer these days is probably to do both. Pupil questions and special interests are listed. Interchange of tradebooks, along with a search for other sources, helps find the answers. Concurrently, the text is read and discussed. If the topic has appeal, and if it is well presented in the text, teacher and pupils may rejoice; the tradebook augmentation and the textbook structure are working together, the two lines of information are conjoining to make a "unit."

At some point, an overall unit structure needs to be developed: the main topics or questions and subtopics that should be covered. Ingenious ways of mapping or charting the structure have been devised, and these tend to be more flexible than the traditional outline. The structure synthesizes textbook topics and items derived from students' interests and their tradebook reading. The structure also helps students distinguish relevant from irrelevant information. For example, a second grader discovers which information from *Koko's Kitten* (Patterson 1987) relates to a discussion about language; a sixth grader extracts ideas about the potential of computers from *Machines That Think* (Asimov et al. 1983).

Incorporating tradebook information into class sessions may require rethinking what a subject-area lesson is all about. Recent attention has been on keeping the lesson tidy: it should not stray from preconceived content objectives; no one should be allowed to "bird walk"; everyone should be "on task." What this translates to in many classrooms is thorough adherence to text: answer all the questions, don't skip anything, and check to see that you remember everything when you're through.

It's easy to debunk such a closed system. It leaves little room for spontaneity. It is not child-centered, hence missing the aura of open-ended learning and self-motivation so dear to proponents of the "open classroom" a decade or so ago. On the other hand, many experienced teachers attest that the debunking is unfair. Objectives *do* need to be set, albeit sometimes with the help of students. Keeping on task and avoiding everyone's tendency sometimes to wander afield are surely necessary.

That is why a text and an overall unit plan are, in my opinion, still important. But to confine the subject-area lesson to text questions and a set of content statements preconceived to be the "knowledge" to be gained from the unit seems to me to negate the greatest goal of education: to inspire the child to *want* to know, to discover that knowledge, orderly or not, is an open system.

One way around the dilemma is to try an equal-time subject-area lesson format. Spend half the period on text, half on tradebook sharing. This necessitates making choices about activities, questions, and subtopics to be omitted from the text. Such omission is compensated *if* you discard items that are clearly unimportant, that are covered anyway in tradebook material, or that are already known to your students. Remember, your content-area text was written with a whole hemisphere as an audience. A class of fourth graders in Puget Sound isn't likely to need to outline, discuss, and recite all the text's material about the seashore. It can turn quickly to tradebooks. But a class based in Kansas may need more text work to establish schema on this topic, though there's likely to be material in other units that your class is already familiar with.

Another way—more daring, more fun, eventually more effective— is to list subtopics and questions at the end of one lesson to be used as the structure for the next lesson. Some of these are derived from the textbook, some from students' suggestions, some from overall unit objectives. All are invitations to seek information from trade-books. The next lesson, then, begins with the pooling of information, discussion of its significance, application of findings through activities, and an evaluation of the "goodness" and utility of the material.

Activities Enhance Discussion

The unit process should not be all reading, talking, and writing answers to questions. Many tradebooks inspire activity if opportunity is given. In a unit on pioneers, three third graders mimed the days-of-the-week chores of homesteaders in 1889, based on their reading of *My Prairie Year* (Harvey 1986). As a spin-off during a fourth-grade science unit on "Light and Lenses," a talented pair assumed the roles of the developers of *The Mirrorstone* (Palin et al. 1986), a fantasy that depends almost entirely upon holograms to entice its readers. Using information including enlarged diagrams from *The Magic of Holography* (Heckman 1986), they demonstrated reflection, refraction, diffraction, and interference with the confidence of experts. M. B. Goffstein's *An Artist* (1980) plus Ernest Raboff's *Marc Chagall* (1988) and *Paul Klee* (1988) produced a mother-daughter demonstration of line-drawing and painting whose payoff could be discerned in the "art appreciation" comments of sixth graders for weeks to come. Activities such as these encourage students to synthesize and apply what they've learned.

Assessment

One type of assessment is to find out what students know about a topic *before* a unit begins. For this purpose, Holmes and Roser (1987) have proposed five assessment techniques: free recall, word association, structured questions, recognition, and unstructured discussion. Findings may indicate that certain vocabulary and concepts taken for granted by text and tradebook must be pre-taught. Findings might also reveal that some or most of the textbook coverage of the topic is already known to most students. Pre-assessment, then, helps determine the balance of text/tradebook emphasis for the unit.

Ongoing assessment—not the "pop quiz" type, but the "let's see if you're understanding this" type—is important throughout the unit. There are often ways to make ongoing assessment a part of the learning experience, not a formal test-taking one. For example, ask students to pose as patriots while you inquire about their reasons for supporting or opposing the Revolution. Tell apprentice oceanographers that they must label seashore specimens and place them in the appropriate habitat on a diagrammed facsimile seashore. Simulation, role-playing, projects that incorporate ad writing, oral direction giving, and any number of synthesizing activities may all be a part of ongoing assessment if we examine results to determine whether students are learning.

Post-assessment is always a problem in regard to curricular topics. If textbook-based, what exactly should be measured? Most teachers know the shallowness of a "facts" test. Many are wary of its opposite—the test of general knowledge that sometimes rewards the student who speaks or writes banalities. Perhaps an alternative is to base post-assessment on the unit structure or outline that has been devised before and during the unit. One phase of assessment is to focus on a subtopic and ask this metalevel question: "What did you learn about this, and how did you learn it?" Ask, too, about the combined effect of textbook and tradebooks: "What did you learn from each of these sources?" From there, post-assessment can sample specific outcomes: vocabulary, basic understanding of content, and application. For the teacher or school system experimenting with a balance between textbook and tradebook sources, post-assessment can help give reassurance that the experiment is worthwhile.

In one study (Long 1984) sixth graders wrote compositions about an imaginary trip to the Soviet Union. Then they read and discussed a group of tradebooks published in Russia for children. Afterwards, they wrote again of an imaginary journey to the Soviet Union. The teacher compared the pre-unit and post-unit results, noting the increase in information and changes in attitude indicated by the compositions. Pre- and post-unit discussions and interviews, taped so that comparison can be easily made, are also recommended by content-area authorities. Hence, a broadened concept of assessment may accompany the broadened view of curricular knowledge fostered by use of tradebooks.

Assess, too, the possibility that use of tradebooks in the curriculum has increased students' interest in reading literature in general. Dulin (1981) provides sample instruments for measuring changes in attitude toward reading. And let us find out whether our attention to tradebooks has increased voluntary reading at school, at home, or anywhere. That may be the most important assessment of all, for voluntary reading gives the key to self-learning long after curricular units are finished.

Recommended Books for Classroom Use

These children's books were also cited as references in the concrete examples for this chapter. An asterisk (*) denotes that a title was listed as out of print when the revised edition of *Using Literature in the Elementary Classroom* went to press.

Ames, Lee J. 1986. *Draw 50 Cars, Trucks, and Motorcycles.* New York: Doubleday.

Asimov, Isaac, Patricia S. Warrick, and Martin H. Greenberg, editors. 1983. *Machines That Think.* New York: Holt.

Banks, Lynne Reid. 1988. *The Indian in the Cupboard.* New York: Camelot.

————. 1988. *The Return of the Indian.* New York: Scholastic.

*Bare, Colleen Stanley. 1985. *Guinea Pigs Don't Read Books.* New York: Dodd, Mead.

Blair, Carvel Hall. 1986. *Exploring the Sea: Oceanography Today.* Illustrated by Harry McNaught. New York: Random House.

*Blumberg, Rhoda. 1983. *The First Travel Guide to the Bottom of the Sea.* New York: Lothrop, Lee and Shepard.

Brown, Osa. 1983. *The Metropolitan Museum of Art Activity Book.* New York: The Metropolitan Museum of Art/Random House.

Collier, James L., and Christopher Collier. 1985. *My Brother Sam Is Dead.* New York: Point.

Demi. 1986. *Demi's Count the Animals One Two Three.* New York: Grosset and Dunlap.

*Edwards, Sally. 1985. *George Midgett's War.* New York: Scribner's.

*Finlayson, Ann. 1972. *Rebecca's War.* New York: Warne.

Forbes, Esther. 1981. *Johnny Tremain.* Boston: Buccaneer.

Fritz, Jean. 1973. *And Then What Happened, Paul Revere?* Illustrated by Margot Tomes. New York: Coward, McCann and Geoghegan.

———. 1982. *Can't You Make Them Behave, King George?* Illustrated by Tomie DePaulo. New York: Coward.

Goffstein, M. B. 1980. *An Artist.* New York: Harper and Row.

———. 1985. *An Artists Album.* New York: Harper and Row.

———. 1987. *Artists' Helpers Enjoy the Evenings.* New York: Harper and Row.

*Harris, Susan. 1979. *The World beneath the Sea.* New York: Watts.

Harvey, Brett. 1986. *My Prairie Year: Based on the Diary of Elenore Plaisted.* Illustrated by Deborah Kogan Ray. New York: Holiday House.

Heckman, Philip. 1986. *The Magic of Holography.* New York: Atheneum.

Henry, Marguerite. 1956. *Cinnabar, the One O'Clock Fox.* Illustrated by Wesley Dennis. New York: Checkerboard.

Holland, Penny. 1986. *Looking at Computer Sounds and Music.* Illustrated by Patti Boyd. New York: Watts.

Jakes, John. 1986. *Susanna of the Alamo: A True Story.* Illustrated by Paul Bacon. San Diego: Gulliver.

*Lauber, Patricia. 1961. *The Story of Numbers.* Illustrated by Mircea Vasiliu. New York: Random House.

*Lawrence, Mildred. 1975. *Touchmark.* New York: Harcourt, Brace, Jovanovich.

Locker, Thomas. 1986. *Sailing with the Wind.* New York: Dial.

Lynn, Sara, and Rosalinda Kightley. 1986. *1 2 3.* Boston: Little, Brown.

Malnig, Anita. 1987. *Where the Waves Break: Life at the Edge of the Sea.* Minneapolis: Lerner.

Marshall, Ray, and John Bradley. 1986. *Train: Watch It Work.* New York: Viking.

Meltzer, Milton. 1986. *George Washington and the Birth of Our Nation.* New York: Watts.

————. 1987. *The American Revolutionaries: A History in Their Own Words.* New York: Crowell.

Mori, Tuyosi. 1986. *Socrates and the Three Little Pigs.* Illustrated by Mitsumasa Anno. New York: Grosset and Dunlap.

Nakano, Dokuihtei. 1986. *Easy Origami.* New York: Viking Kestrel.

Palin, Michael, Alan Lee, and Richard Seymour. 1986. *The Mirrorstone.* New York: Knopf.

Patterson, Francine. 1987. *Koko's Kitten.* Photos by Ronald H. Cohn. New York: Scholastic.

Prokofiev, Sergei. 1986. *Peter and the Wolf.* Retold by Loriot, with pictures by Jörg Müller. New York: Knopf.

Raboff, Ernest. 1988. *Marc Chagall.* New York: Trophy.

————. 1988. *Paul Klee.* New York: Trophy.

Rinard, Judith E. 1986. *Dolphins: Our Friends in the Sea.* Washington, D.C.: The National Geographic Society.

Roop, Peter, and Connie Roop. 1987. *Buttons for General Washington.* Illustrated by Peter E. Hanson. Minneapolis: Lerner.

Sattler, Helen Roney. 1985. *Sharks, the Super Fish.* Illustrated by Jean Day Zallinger. New York: Lothrop, Lee and Shepard.

Schwartz, David M. 1987. *How Much Is a Million?* Illustrated by Steven Kellogg. New York: Scholastic.

Settle, Mary Lee. 1984. *Water World.* New York: Lodestar.

Strand, Mark. 1986. *Rembrandt Takes a Walk.* Illustrated by Red Grooms. New York: Crown.

Ventura, Piero. 1984. *Great Painters.* New York: Putnam.

*Weiss, Malcolm E. 1976. *666 Jellybeans! All That?* Illustrated by Judith Hoffman Corwin. New York: Crowell.

West, Robin. 1987. *Far Out: How to Create Your Own Star World.* Minneapolis: Carolrhoda.

References

Anderson, Richard C., E. H. Hiebert, J. A. Scott, I. A. G. Wilkinson. 1985. *Becoming a Nation of Readers.* Washington, D.C.: National Academy of Education.

Banks, James A., and Ambrose A. Clegg, Jr. 1985. *Teaching Strategies for the Social Studies.* 3d ed. New York: Longman.

Betza, Ruth. 1987. Evaluating Computer Books with the Yawn Index. *Reading Horizons* 28:26–33.

Burton, Frederick R. 1986. Research Currents: A Teacher's Conception of the Action Research Process. *Language Arts* 63:718–23.

Davis, James E., editor. 1979. *Dealing with Censorship.* Urbana, Ill.: National Council of Teachers of English.

Dulin, Ken L. 1981. Assessing Reading Interests of Elementary and Middle School Students. In *Developing Active Readers: Ideas for Parents, Teachers, and Librarians,* edited by Dianne L. Monson and DayAnn K. McClenathan, 2–15. Newark, Del.: International Reading Association.

Gillespie, John T., and Christine Gilbert. 1985. *Best Books for Children.* 3d ed. New York: Bowker.

Hickman, Janet. 1986. Bookwatching. *Language Arts* 63:85–93.

Holmes, Betty C., and Nancy L. Roser. 1987. Five Ways to Assess Readers' Prior Knowledge. *The Reading Teacher* 40:646–49.

Long, Roberta. 1984. Soviet Children's Books: Expanding Children's Views of the Soviet Union. *Journal of Reading* 27:418–22.

Rosenblatt, Louise M. 1938, 1968. *Literature as Exploration.* East Norwalk, Conn.: Appleton-Century.

Sebesta, Sam L. 1987. Enriching the Arts and Humanities through Children's Books. In *Children's Books in the Reading Program,* edited by Bernice E. Cullinan, 28–37. Newark, Del.: International Reading Association.

Southgate, Vera, H. Arnold, and S. Johnson. 1981. *Extending Beginning Reading.* London: Heinemann.

Subject Guide to Children's Books in Print 1986–1987. 1986. New York: Bowker.

Sutherland, Zena, and May Hill Arbuthnot. 1986. *Children and Books.* 7th ed. Glenview, Ill.: Scott, Foresman.

Veatch, Jeanette. 1968. *Reading in the Elementary School.* New York: John Wiley.

Woolsey, Daniel R., and Frederick R. Burton. 1986. Blending Literary and Informational Ways of Knowing. *Language Arts* 63:273–80.

Related Readings

Monson, Dianne L., editor. 1985. *Adventuring with Books.* Urbana, Ill.: National Council of Teachers of English.

This ambitious volume recommends 1,700 children's books, published between 1981 and 1984. Major headings include curricular areas (science, social studies, fine arts, sports) as well as genres (poetry, biography, modern fantasy). The reviews are of mixed origin but most are directed to teachers and librarians who consider a book's appeal to children, along with its "literary and artistic quality." There are many uses for a compendium such as this. One use might be to prove to subject-area specialists that a substantial selection of current tradebooks *is* extant, relevant to their fields. Another use, perhaps surprising, is for browsing: reading *about* books can be as pleasant and purposeful as reading recipes.

Moore, David W., Sharon Arthur Moore, Patricia M. Cunningham, and James W. Cunningham. 1986. *Developing Readers and Writers in the Content Areas: K–12.* New York: Longman.

Nine "essential thinking processes" described in the opening chapter could justify and guide the use of tradebooks in curricular teaching. The fourth chapter compares content-area literature and textbooks, speculating that the former may be "better written, more interesting" and citing examples on the topic of ancient Greece. To help organize a unit encompassing both types of material, the authors suggest a "curriculum web," a comprehensive diagram that includes tradebook titles and activities (see pages 92, 93). The latter third of this emphasis-on-application text is in journal form: teachers of grade one, grade five, and of selected subject areas at the secondary level narrate their year-long classroom activities, integrating text and trade materials.

Editors

Sam Leaton Sebesta is a professor of education (reading/language arts) at the University of Washington in Seattle. Before joining the university faculty, he taught grades one through six. He has co-authored numerous textbooks for elementary and college students, and for several years has been the children's review editor for *The Reading Teacher*. As co-chair for the Children's Choices project, Sebesta has studied children's reading interests and published numerous research studies on that topic.

John Warren Stewig, a former elementary schoolteacher of kindergarten through grade six, now is a professor in the Department of Curriculum and Instruction at the University of Wisconsin–Milwaukee. He chaired the NCTE National Conference on Language Arts in the Elementary School, held in Phoenix in 1977, and was president of NCTE in 1982. Recently Stewig published *Children and Literature* and *The Fisherman and His Wife*, a retelling of a folktale for children. In 1987 the University of Wisconsin–Madison named him its distinguished elementary education alumnus of the year.

Contributors

Helen Felsenthal is director of special education in the Graduate School of Education at the University of Pennsylvania. From 1973 to 1978 she was the language arts program coordinator at Research for Better Schools, a federally funded research and development laboratory in Philadelphia. Previously she served on the language arts faculty at Purdue University, taught elementary classes, and was a counselor and school psychologist. Felsenthal is an author in Houghton Mifflin's ENGLISH basal series and contributed a chapter to the 1988 edition of *Teaching Reading: Foundations and Strategies*.

Mary Jett-Simpson is an associate professor of reading/language arts education in the Department of Curriculum and Instruction at the University of Wisconsin–Milwaukee. She has served on the NCTE Elementary Section Committee and is currently editing *Adventuring with Books*. In addition to journal articles, book chapters, and a third-grade language arts textbook, Jett-Simpson was the major developer and writer of the inservice series "Teaching Reading Comprehension," distributed by the Agency for Instructional Technology.

Richard G. Kolczynski is a professor of English education at Ball State University, where he teaches courses in language arts, children's literature, reading, and research in English education. He has taught in elementary schools and now serves as a consultant to several school systems. He also has served on several NCTE committees and was a member of the Elementary Section Steering Committee and the Review Board of *Language Arts*. Kolczynski was program chair of the elementary strand for the 1986 NCTE Spring Conference.

Alden J. Moe is dean of the College of Education at Lehigh University. Formerly an elementary classroom teacher, a secondary reading teacher, and a reading consultant, he also has been on the faculty of Purdue University and Louisiana State University. He is co-author of *Analytical Reading Inventory* (fourth edition), *The Vocabulary of First Grade Children*, and *The Ginn Word Book for Teachers: A Basic Lexicon*. Moe also is the senior author of the *Keystones for Reading* series. He has developed computer software for the analysis of text; these programs were used to analyze the vocabularies of the books that are recommended in his chapter of this volume.

A. Barbara Pilon is a professor in the Languages and Literature Department at Worcester State College in Worcester, Massachusetts. She edits all professional book reviews for *Gifted Child Quarterly;* she has served as secretary and recording secretary for the National Association for Gifted Children and was a board member of NAGC for more than twenty years. Among Pilon's publications are a volume of poetry, *Concrete Is Not Always Hard;* a textbook, *Teaching Language Arts Creatively in the Elementary Grades;* and "Dialects and Reading: Implications for Change," presented at the Elementary Language Arts Conference, 1975, and available on cassette from NCTE.